Miniature Embroidery
for the Victorian Dolls' House

Miniature Embroidery
for the Victorian Dolls' House

Pamela Warner

Guild of Master Craftsman Publications Ltd

First published 1998 by
Guild of Master Craftsman Publications Ltd,
166 High Street, Lewes,
East Sussex, BN7 1XU

© Pamela Warner 1998

ISBN 1 86108 095 6

Photography and cover photograph by Zul Mukhida

Charts produced by Peter Rhodes

Black-and-white line drawings by John Yates, from sketches by Pamela Warner,
except drawings in the Stitch Glossary, by Pamela Warner

Colour drawings and patterns by Pamela Warner

Designed by Teresa Dearlove

Typeface: Perpetua

Colour origination by Viscan Graphics (Singapore)
Printed and bound by Kyodo Printing (Singapore) under the supervision of
MRM Graphics, Winslow, Buckinghamshire, UK

Introduction   1

1   Influences on design and style   2

THE PROJECTS

2   Carpets   10

3   Rugs   25

4   Curtains   36

5   Cushions, chair seats and footstools   57

6   Screens   94

7   Table covers and linen   108

8   Pictures and samplers   113

9   Bedcovers   122

10   Small decorative items   145

TECHNIQUES

11   Working to 1/24 scale   161

12   Frames and transfer of designs   164

13   Bonding methods and colouring techniques   169

14   Finishing methods   172

Stitch glossary   174

Sources of information   181

About the author   183

Index   184

Contents

For Bunny

Note on Measurements

Throughout, measurements are given in both metric and imperial systems. Please use only one system for each project as the two are equivalents only and are not exact.

For 'materials required', imperial measurements have been rounded up to the nearest ½in as shops will not sell to the ⅛ or ¹⁄₁₆in.

MANY miniaturists choose to set their houses in a general Tudor, Jacobean, Georgian or Victorian era, which allows a large degree of freedom within the chosen period. Each of these eras spanned many years, during which there were many changes in styles and living conditions.

Having had a life-long interest in model making I 'discovered' dolls' houses in 1990. All my houses are furnished and decorated to a particular date, reflecting my interest in social history. I have been teaching embroidery for 20 years and writing about and teaching the history of embroidery for almost as long. Naturally, because of this, any needlework or textiles that I made for my houses needed to be of the right design or technique for the period.

I soon found, after admitting to being a 'dolls' house addict', that many of my friends and students were secret miniaturists too. We formed the Orpington Doll's House and Miniaturists Society. Some of us began to design and make our own dolls' houses, using skills we acquired on a dolls' house holiday in Stafford, under the expert tuition of Peter Alden.

My knowledge of textile history was soon in demand and I thought, why not a book on miniature embroidery? This volume, covering Victorian and Edwardian styles, will be followed by one on the Georgian period and then by two more on Tudor and Jacobean styles and the Twentieth Century.

My objective is to help miniaturists who wish to be more specific with the date of the furnishings of their dolls' houses or room settings, with this book aimed at showing the appropriate design and style of needlework for the Victorian and Edwardian eras.

Although it would be acceptable to include furnishings of an earlier time, which could have been handed down through the family, it is desirable to avoid any item which is later than the chosen period.

I hope that the projects in this book will provide enjoyment for all embroiderers and stitchers, whether they are beginners or experienced, and whether they have a dolls' house, room box or just want a tiny carpet on which to display a treasure.

Introduction

1 Influences on design and style

The nineteenth century saw the flowering of a new middle class — wealthy families who were in business, industry or trade — from the merchant class of the previous century. The Victorians continued to build prestigious houses, in both town and country, as did their predecessors. Their homes were furnished with a high degree of comfort, giving a deliberate outward show of wealth.

The wives and daughters of these wealthy gentlemen maintained this show of status by being seen not to engage in anything that appeared to be work. However, it was also unseemly for such ladies to appear to be idle. As good causes and needlework were the only respectable alternatives, this resulted in an abundance of needlework to fill all available time and space.

The poor would have had very little, if any, comforts. Any needlework in their homes was purely functional, with little decoration. Patchwork items, for example, were simple shapes of surviving fabric scraps sewn together without too much regard for design or decoration. Higher up the social scale a greater degree of ornamentation was evident.

In large houses, furnishings varied from room to room. The most opulent were on display in the 'public' rooms (dining and drawing rooms) with less showy but very comfortable furnishings in 'private' rooms (the ladies' sitting room and bedrooms) and very basic items in the servants' quarters. However, in a very wealthy house, the owner would take pride in the fact that his upper servants also had some degree of comfort, and would show this by dressing them rather well. For example, the female staff would have uniforms trimmed with modest lace.

There were many magazines available to fuel the huge demand for embroidery and needlework. These all contained charts, patterns and, after 1874, transfers. Prepared items such as coloured charts, materials and trimmings were also available, from haberdashery shops.

Early Victorian (1837–1860)

The influence of the neo-classical period continued into the beginning of the nineteenth century. A light and elegant style, with swathes and garlands of flowers linked with ribbon bows, or arranged in classical vases or urns. Delicate colours were popular, touched with gold.

The 1840s heralded the Gothic Revival, with the leading designers looking back to Mediaeval times for inspiration. This, in turn, inspired William Morris and his contemporaries, and led to the development of the Arts and Crafts Movement.

From the 1830s, ladies began embroidering Berlin Wool Work: canvaswork using tent stitch (petit point) or cross stitch (gros point). The designs were copied from coloured charts using Berlin wool. Both the charts and the wool were originally produced in and around the area of Berlin, but from 1831 they were produced and sold throughout Europe and North America.

The early charts were hand coloured and well designed, often with delicate flowers and motifs. Copies of well-known paintings and biblical scenes were also popular. The wools were coloured using natural dyes until 1856, when chemical dyes became available.

Victorian ladies used Berlin Wool Work on carpets, pole and hand screens, sofas, cushions, bell pulls, waistcoats, slippers, braces, bags, watch pockets, covers, mantel and curtain trims and almost anything else they could think of. In fact, the work was so widespread that some books of the time called it just 'needlework' as if no other technique existed.

Fig 1.1 **Hand coloured Berlin Wool Work chart, 1840s, produced by A. Todt of Berlin.**

Fig 1.2 **Berlin Wool Work watch pocket with grisaille beads, 1860s.**

Late Victorian (1860–1901)

With the advent of chemical dyes, Berlin Wool Work was produced with harsh, vibrant colours – magenta, purple and bright greens. They were used with great enthusiasm, if not much taste or judgement.

By this time the number of needlework magazines had increased, and they now had printed colour charts, inferior in both colour and design to the earlier hand coloured ones. The designs varied from floral posies and wreaths to copies of popular paintings and even such subjects as the Prince of Wales as a baby, with various royal dogs, on a tartan rug.

Some of the charts were worked in plush stitch. This stitch gives a raised, tufted effect, and is mostly used for flowers, but also to highlight areas in exuberant pictures, for example, a parrot perched on a vase or urn. A similar effect to plush stitch can be achieved with velvet stitch. In the late 1860s and early 1870s geometric, all-over patterns were used widely on upholstery and furnishings.

In the early 1870s there was a reaction against the harsh Berlin Wool Work and the inferior designs. The soft, faded colours returned to favour as a great interest in antique needlework developed. Art Needlework began to take over and became very popular. This beautiful silk embroidery imitates nature realistically – it is almost like painting with the needle. Transfers were readily available with suitable designs for all manner of household items.

Samplers from this time were very much a school room exercise, usually verses or alphabets with simple motifs, and sometimes in limited colour. The Berlin Wool Work sampler, however, was a long narrow strip, being a record of patterns and motifs to be rolled up in the workbox and used for future reference.

Patchwork and quilting were worked throughout the Victorian era. Patchwork and appliqué pictures were particularly popular during the 1870s and crazy patchwork was widely used for bed coverings, sofa and piano throws, and gentlemen's dressing gowns.

Fig 1.3 **Berlin Wool Work cushion, late 1870s.**

Arts and Crafts Style (1870s onwards)

The Arts and Crafts style developed from the Gothic Revival of the 1840s and 1850s, which itself looked back to Mediaeval craftsmen and designers for inspiration.

William Morris was one of the principal designers of the Arts and Crafts movement. He believed that people should have handmade, well-designed items in their home and not the mass-produced, machine-made furnishings that he disliked so much.

Much of his design work was based on early tapestries and hangings, featuring curly acanthus leaves, flowers, birds and animals. He worked closely with other designers, including Walter Crane and Edward Burne-Jones who were both noted for their skilled figure drawing.

Fig 1.4 **Motif from a curtain worked in twisted silk, 1880s–90s. (The net overlay is to conserve the fragile fabric.)**

Art Nouveau Style (Late 1890s–1910)

This style developed through the Pre-Raphaelite and Arts and Crafts movements, and was popular throughout Europe and North America. The main characteristics of the style are the extended flowing lines of the designs.

In Britain the style was centred in Glasgow, led by Charles Rennie Mackintosh and the Glasgow School of Art. In England Walter Crane and Christopher Dresser were foremost in developing the trend. Paris and Vienna were the other main centres, each with its own characteristics and designers.

The Edwardian Era (1901–1910)

In this period, the upper class house continued to display all the trappings of wealth that the Victorians loved so much. However, the Edwardian era had an added elegance and quality reflecting both the

Fig 1.5 **Panel of Art Needlework, 1890s.**

Fig 1.6 **Pair of mats with lace trimmings and Art Needlework motifs, c.1910.**

Art Nouveau influence and the Aesthetic movement. The latter developed from an interest in Japanese artifacts which were imported into Britain from the late 1870s and made popular by Liberty and Co., the well-known London store.

The style was typified by textiles and embroidery in pale greys and mauves with an Oriental feel to the design. Main reception rooms and bedrooms were often furnished with Oriental-style pieces and decorated with Oriental-style panels painted on the walls.

Nineteenth and Early Twentieth Century Styles

Date	Period	Reigning monarch	
1760–1812	Late Georgian	George III	
1812–1820	Regency	George III	
1820–1830	Late Regency	George IV	
1830–1837	William IV	William IV	
1837–1860	Early Victorian	Victoria	
1860–1901	Late Victorian	Victoria	(Arts and Crafts: c.1880–1920)
1901–1910	Edwardian	Edward VII	(Art Nouveau: c.1890–1910)

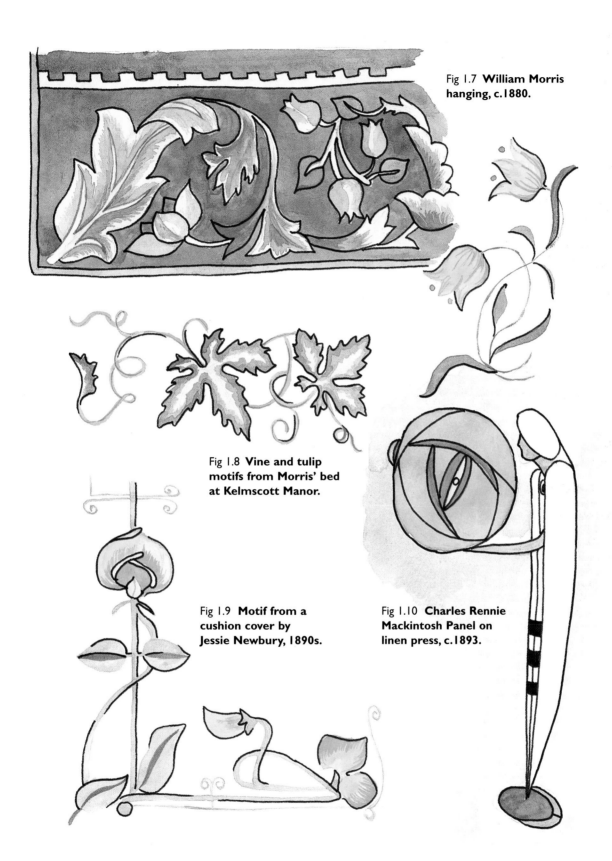

Fig 1.7 **William Morris hanging, c.1880.**

Fig 1.8 **Vine and tulip motifs from Morris' bed at Kelmscott Manor.**

Fig 1.9 **Motif from a cushion cover by Jessie Newbury, 1890s.**

Fig 1.10 **Charles Rennie Mackintosh Panel on linen press, c.1893.**

The Projects

The projects are all presented in 1/12 scale as this is the most popular. Instructions for working to 1/24 scale are basically the same, but a table of approximate sizes, alternative fabrics and the number of threads to use is given in Chapter 11. Patterns can be reduced on a photocopier.

If you use a canvas or evenweave other than those suggested, divide the number of stitches along the length and width of the chart by the number of threads per inch of the fabric to find the finished size of your carpet in inches. To convert this to millimetres, multiply the final number by 25.4.

The designs for most of the projects are based on existing examples or contemporary paintings. The resulting designs have been simplified to allow for the reduction in scale, but retain the feel of the particular period.

Each square on the chart represents one stitch over one thread of the canvas. Refer to the photographs of the completed items if in doubt.

It is possible to have a design photocopied, in colour, directly onto the canvas. Details of this option are given in Chapter 12 (*see* page 168).

The materials and threads used are all readily available: any good needlework magazine, trade or telephone directory will list mail order suppliers and retailers. Equivalent colour numbers for the main brands of threads are given, with the nearest alternative listed, where an exact match is not possible.

Both metric and imperial measurements are given. In any individual project use *either* the metric *or* the imperial measurements, not a mixture of both, as the conversions are equivalents only.

Early Victorian room setting.

2 Carpets

During the late eighteenth century and into the early nineteenth century it was fashionable to colour, stencil or pattern wooden or solid floors instead of using a carpet. Oiled floor cloths, coloured and patterned in the same way, were also popular, often forming a surround even when a central carpet was used. These oil cloths usually imitated marble, stone or even wood. Linoleum, developed around the mid-nineteenth century, was widely used by the time of the Edwardian era.

From the mid-nineteenth century, carpets came to be in more general use. Modest rooms would have a small carpet or rug near the fireplace and larger rooms, especially those used for entertaining, would have a larger central carpet, or even one that almost fitted the room. Such large carpets would often have a central patterned area and a decorative border around the edge.

Finishing the carpets

To finish the edges of the carpets, the third row of the pattern must be worked through the hem. Therefore, remember not to work this row initially. (*See* page 18.)

You may need to block your carpet if the shape has distorted during stitching. Do this before completing the edges, as you will need the extra canvas around the edges to pin the carpet out to shape. Instructions for this process are given in Chapter 14 (*see* page 172).

Fig 2.1 **Early Victorian carpet, based on an embroidered carpet made during the 1840s.**

Early Victorian Carpet

This design is based on an embroidered carpet made during the 1840s which itself imitated the design of the fashionable, but very expensive, imported woven and knotted carpets. These usually featured a wide border built up from smaller bands of pattern, with a central motif on a patterned background.

The colouring used makes this carpet equally suited to an Edwardian parlour, study or library.

Early Victorian Carpet

Materials
Stranded cotton as listed in colour key

Coin net (24 count): 250 x 200mm
    (10 x 8in) OR

Mono canvas (22 count): 250 x 200mm
    (10 x 8in)

Tapestry needle: No. 26

Size
174 x 118 stitches

Coin net (24 count): 187 x 127mm (7⅜ x 5in)

Mono canvas (22 count): 200 x 147mm (7⅞ x 5¾in)

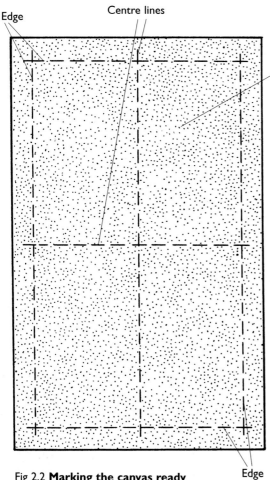

Edge   Centre lines

Canvas

Edge

Fig 2.2 **Marking the canvas ready for use. Broken lines show tacking stitches marking the vertical and horizontal centres and the outline of the embroidered area.**

Preparation

Prepare the canvas by marking the centre lines and outside edge with tacking stitches. Mount the canvas in a rectangular frame as shown in Chapter 12 (*see* page 165).

Working method

Beginning either in the centre or on the outer edge, follow the chart, using two strands of stranded cotton in tent stitch.

Do not work the third row in from the edge until you are making up the carpet. This row is worked through the turned edge of the canvas to hold the hem in place. A fringe can be added to each end of the carpet if desired (*see* page 19).

Early Victorian Carpet

		Skeins	DMC	Anchor	Madeira
	Deep red	2	815	20	0512
	Scarlet	1	321	47	0509
	Blue	2	797	139	0912
	Green	2	937	268	1504
	Beige	1	841	388	1910
	White	1	Blanc	White	White
	Black	1	310	403	Black

Fig 2.3 **Chart for early Victorian carpet.**

Fig 2.4 **Late Victorian carpet.**

Late Victorian Carpet

This design is taken from a painting of an 1880s room and reflects the lighter colouring popular at that time. It has a wide floral border, with a simple geometric pattern filling the centre.

The pale green background shown here can be replaced with powder blue, light dusty pink or light fawn if preferred.

Preparation

Prepare the canvas by marking the centre lines and edges with tacking stitches. Mount the canvas in a rectangular frame as shown in Chapter 12 (*see* page 165).

Working method

It is easier for this design to begin with the outer borders, working along an end and a side

Late Victorian Carpet

Materials	Size
Stranded cotton as listed in colour key	192 x 132 stitches
Coin net (24 count): 290 x 230mm	Coin net (24 count): 212 x 147mm ($8\frac{5}{16}$ x $5\frac{3}{4}$in)
(11 x 9in) OR	Mono canvas (22 count): 246 x 170mm ($9\frac{11}{16}$ x $6\frac{11}{16}$in)
Mono canvas (22 count): 290 x 230mm	
(11 x 9in)	
Tapestry needle: No. 26	

Late Victorian Carpet		Skeins	DMC	Anchor	Madeira
	Pale yellow	1	744	301	0112
	Dark green	2	502	876	1703
	Red	1	817	13	0212
	Dark pink	1	221	1019	0810
	Mid pink	2	223	895	0812
Alternative backgrounds					
	Light green (on chart)	5	504	1024	1701
	Powder blue	5	809	39	0508
	Light dusty pink	5	778	1016	0809
	Light fawn	5	842	388	1910

first. Follow the chart, using two strands of stranded cotton in tent stitch.

Do not work the third row in from the edge until you are making up the carpet. This row is worked through the turned edge of the canvas to hold the hem in place. A fringe can be added to each end if required (*see* page 19).

Fig 2.5 **Chart for late Victorian carpet.**

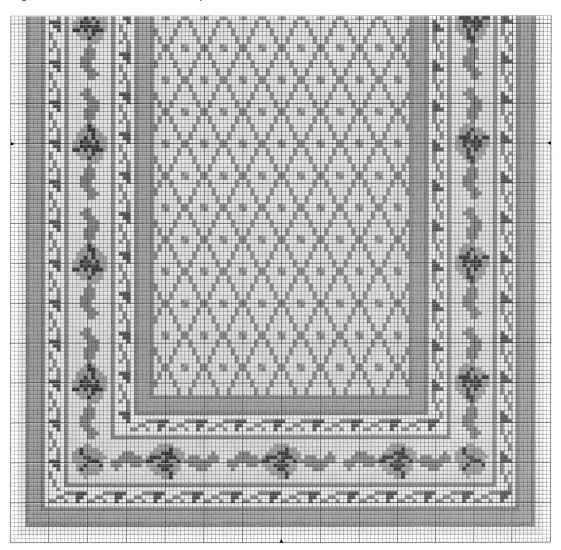

15

Fig 2.6 **Arts and Crafts carpet.**

Arts and Crafts Movement Carpet

This carpet is based on a design by William Morris, c.1880, which he produced for use by his company, Morris and Co.

Preparation

Prepare the canvas by marking the centre lines and the outside edge with tacking stitches. Mount the canvas in a rectangular frame as shown in Chapter 12 (*see* page 165).

Arts and Crafts Movement Carpet

Materials

Stranded cotton as listed in colour key

A Coin net (24 count): 250 x 150mm
   (10 x 6in) OR

B Mono canvas (22 count): 250 x 150mm
   (10 x 6in) OR

C Mono canvas (18 count): 300 x 180mm
   (12 x 7in)

D Mono canvas (14 count): 370 x 220mm
   (14½in x 8¾in)

Tapestry needle for:

   A No. 26

   B No. 24

   C No. 24

   D No. 24

Size

As this is a smaller carpet, alternative sizes for larger versions on different canvases have been given.

162 x 82 stitches

A Coin net (24 count): 178 x 90mm (7 x 3½in)

B Mono canvas: (22 count) 188 x 103mm (7⅜ x 4in)

C Mono canvas: (18 count) 230 x 115mm (9 x 4½in)

D Mono canvas: (14 count) 290 x 150mm
   (11⅜ x 5⅞in)

Arts and Crafts Movement Carpet

		Skeins A & B	C	D	DMC	Anchor	Madeira
	Stone	2	3	5	739	372	2013
	Gold	1	1	1	783	307	2211
	Green	1	2	3	471	280	1501
	Red	1	1	1	815	20	0512
	Light blue	1	1	1	519	1038	1105
	Orange	1	1	1	970	304	0202
	Dark blue	3	5	8	939	152	1009

Fig 2.7 **Chart for Arts and Crafts carpet.**

Working method

Follow the chart using tent stitch throughout. For the coin net and 22 count mono canvas use two strands of stranded cotton, for the 18 count mono canvas use three strands and for the 14 count use six strands.

Do not work the third row in from the edge until you are making the carpet up. This row is worked through the turned edge of the canvas to hold the hem in place. A fringe can be added to each end if desired (*see* page 19).

Finishing hems

Preparation

If the carpet has distorted during working, you will need to stretch and block it *before* finishing the hem. Instructions for blocking are given in Chapter 14 (*see* page 172). Blocking must be done before the edges are turned under and worked.

Working method

1 Trim the canvas down to six threads all round the edge of the piece, and remove a little canvas from each corner.
2 Fold the corner under diagonally as shown in Fig 2.8.
3 Fold each edge under, close to the stitching, to form a mitred corner.
4 Now work the missing row of tent stitch (the third row) through both layers. The holes in both layers should line up.

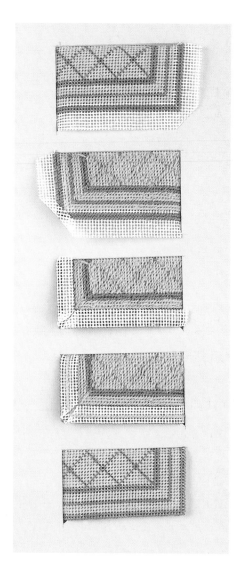

Fig 2.8 **Finishing a hem.**

5 Trim the surplus canvas back to the hem.
6 If necessary, leave the carpet face down under a weight – possibly a heavy book – for a couple of days. This is better than pressing with an iron, which will produce a ridge on the right side and flatten the embroidery along the hems.
7 A fringe can be added to each end of any carpet or rug if desired.

Miniature Fringes

There are two methods that can be used for making miniature fringes. The first uses a strip of fabric, which is frayed at the edges to give a fringe effect. Almost any fine fabric can be used, for example, silk, cotton and linen.

In the second method a knotted edge is made from fine cord or embroidery thread.

Working methods for fringes

Fabric fringes

1 Cut a strip of fabric 50–60mm (2–2⅜in) wide, and 100mm (4in) longer than the required length of the finished fringe.

2 Work two rows of straight machine stitching, close together, down the approximate centre of the strip, following the grain of the fabric. The sample in Fig 2.9 was stitched in a contrasting thread for clarity.

3 Trim the upper edge of the fabric close to the machine stitching.

4 Machine a row of close, zig zag stitches over the straight stitching, enclosing the top edge. A narrow braid or ribbon or a Perlé embroidery cotton (No. 5 or 3) could be added at this stage by passing it under the foot of the machine and laying it over the straight stitching. The zig zag, which can be more open if this addition is made, will then incorporate the thread.

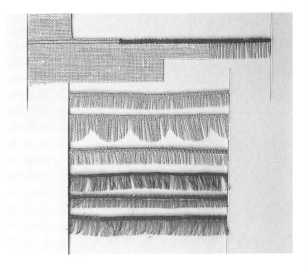

Fig 2.9 **Making a fabric fringe.**

5 Trim the lower edge of the fabric to the desired width of the fringe. For a straight edge, use the grain of the fabric as a guide. Alternatively, a scalloped or shaped fringe can be made. To do this, lightly draw the desired shape along the length of the fabric, in pencil or fabric pen, and cut along that line.

6 Fray the fabric back to the stitching, removing one thread at a time. If you pull too many away at once, the fringe distorts.

7 Stitch or glue the fringe in place on the completed item. If you use PVA fabric glue, use only a minimal amount. Avoid ordinary household glues, some of which may discolour and become sticky with time.

Knotted fringes

1 Turn under the edge of the fabric or canvas.

2 Cut the thread or cord into lengths; about 100mm (4in) is manageable.

3 Fold these lengths in half and pull them through the edge of the hem with a fine crochet hook to form a loop (*see* Fig 2.10).

19

Fig 2.10 **Making a knotted fringe.**

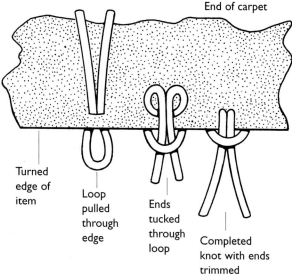

End of carpet

Turned edge of item

Loop pulled through edge

Ends tucked through loop

Completed knot with ends trimmed

4 Slip the two ends of the thread down through the loop, and pull them firmly to tighten the knot.

5 Trim the threads to the desired length for the fringe when the whole row of knots has been completed.

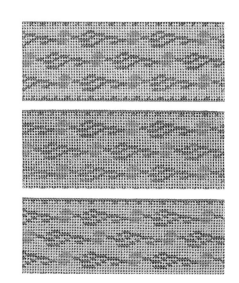

Fig 2.11 **Stair carpets. Left to right: Design A, Design B, Design C.**

Stair Carpets

Prior to the nineteenth century, staircases in upper class houses were elegant and grand. They were often marble with balusters of ornate iron or finely turned wood – three to each stair. These grand staircases were not always covered with a carpet. In smaller houses, the staircases were wooden, with slender, intricately shaped balusters (two to a stair) and narrow handrails. Towards the end of the eighteenth century, however, simpler shapes became fashionable.

By the nineteenth century, staircases were much simpler, usually with an oval handrail. Many houses had an additional rear staircase, often without access to windows and with a skylight at most. The main staircase of the house usually had carpet held in place with brass rods, while upper or rear staircases were either left bare, or given a simple covering, more to muffle sound than to provide comfort.

The Designs

Three designs are given, each shown in three colourways. Design A, with its darker background colours, is suitable for early to mid-Victorian houses, and also for Edwardian houses. Design B, with light coloured backgrounds, suits late Victorian houses, though with a darker background substituted it would suit an Arts and Crafts house. Design C, with its elongated floral motif, is ideal for the Art Nouveau house. You can, of course, use any background colour you choose.

Calculating carpet length

To find the exact length of carpet required, cut a strip of paper 50–60mm (2–2⅜in) wide and 600–700mm (23⅝–27¾in) long. Beginning at the foot of the staircase, place the end of the strip level with the floor. Carefully fold the paper into the contours of each tread and riser until you reach the top. This will give you the finished length required.

If you find the finished carpet is a little short on the stairs, it is possible to work a little more out of the frame.

Stair Carpets

Materials
Stranded cotton as listed in colour key
Tapestry needle: No. 24
Designs A and B
Mono interlock canvas (18 count): 150mm (6in) x required length + 100mm (4in)
Design C
Mono interlock canvas (18 count): 140mm (5½in) x required length + 100mm (4in)

Size
Designs A and B
37 x 9 stitches per pattern repeat
Pattern repeat per stair: 27 rows
Mono interlock canvas (18 count): 52mm (2¹⁄₁₆in) wide
Design C
30 x 27 stitches per pattern repeat
Pattern repeat per two stairs: 54 rows
Mono interlock canvas (18 count): 42mm (1⅝in) wide

Preparation

Mark the length and width on the canvas with tacking stitches. Mount the canvas in a rectangular frame or stretcher as shown in Chapter 12 (*see* page 165).

All the examples have been worked on mono interlock canvas (18 count) because it is more pliable than other materials and will bend to the stairs more easily.

Allow at least 50mm (2in) each side and a similar amount at each end. This will help to keep the piece in shape, and if the completed piece has still distorted, this turning will be needed to stretch it into shape.

Stair Carpet – Design A

		Skeins	DMC	Anchor	Madeira
	Light green	4	471	280	1501
	Light pink	2	224	893	0404
	Dark pink	1	223	895	0812

Alternative backgrounds

		Skeins	DMC	Anchor	Madeira
	Deep red (on chart)	4	902	22	0514
	Dark green	4	937	268	1504
	Dark blue	4	939	152	1009

Stair Carpet – Design B

		Skeins	DMC	Anchor	Madeira
	Dark green	3	502	876	1703
	Red	1	817	13	0212

Alternative backgrounds

		Skeins	DMC	Anchor	Madeira
	Cream(on chart)	5	3047	956	2109
	Green	5	504	1024	1701
	Beige	5	841	388	1910

Stair Carpet – Design C

		Skeins	DMC	Anchor	Madeira
	Dark green	2	502	876	1703
	Deep peach	1	352	9	0303
	Yellow	1	725	293	0110

Alternative backgrounds

		Skeins	DMC	Anchor	Madeira
	Biscuit (on chart)	4	739	372	2013
	Light green	4	504	1024	1701
	Peach	4	945	367	2013

Fig 2.12 **Chart for stair carpet, Design A.**

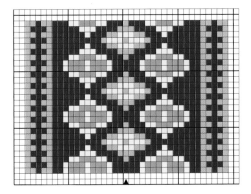

Fig 2.13 **Chart for stair carpet, Design B.**

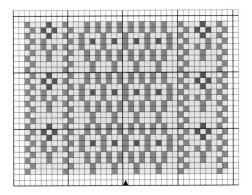

Fig 2.14 **Chart for stair carpet, Design C.**

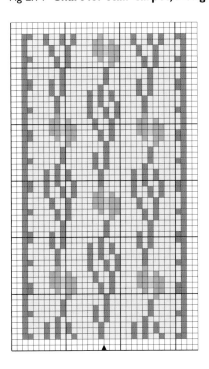

Working method

Follow the required chart using tent stitch with three strands of stranded cotton throughout.

Do not work the third row in from each edge until you are making up the carpet (*see* page 18).

Trim the side edges back to 25mm (1in) when turning and working the hem, and cut away any surplus canvas when the hem is finished.

Quantities of thread given are for an average length of stair carpet to fit a standard straight staircase, i.e. 55cm (22in).

Fitting a stair carpet

To fit a completed stair carpet, either use miniature stair rods and fit as directed by the maker, or use the following method. Take your time and deal with each stair one at a time for an excellent result.

Working method

1 Fold the lower edge of unworked canvas under and lightly glue with PVA.

2 When dry, glue this lower edge to the bottom riser, level with the floor, and leave to dry.

3 Place a line of glue into the rear angle of the first tread (indicated by the arrow in Fig 2.15).

4 Carefully push the carpet into the angle using a firm edge. A cut-down old credit card is ideal. Hold it in place until the glue 'grips' and allow to dry completely before proceeding with the next stair. This will give a good flat fit to each stair.

5 Repeat the process for each individual stair

23

Fig 2.15 **Fitting a stair carpet.**

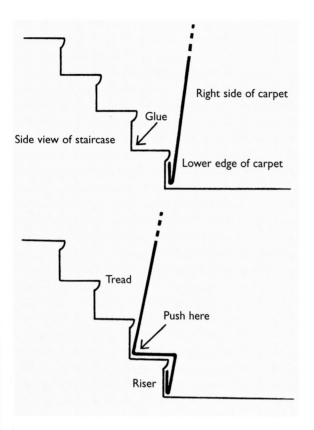

until they are all covered.

6 Turn the unworked canvas under at the top and glue as in step 1.

7 Secure the carpet to the top step or take it under a landing carpet if required.

3 Rugs

Small, plain and utilitarian rugs were used in the less important rooms of an upper class house – in front of the fire or by the bed for example. They were also used throughout smaller houses, often in rooms where the main floor was either of bare boards or linoleum.

Decorative tufted or embroidered rugs were used, when required, in the more public rooms of larger houses.

Late Victorian room setting.

Fig 3.1 **Couched rugs.
From left: chenille; soft
rayon cord; Perlé cotton.**

Couched Rugs

Preparation

Select the size required from Fig 3.2 or draw your own pattern to any size or shape you like. Mark the shape, including the centre line, onto a piece of fine cotton fabric that is large enough

to fit a frame. If the pattern has been drawn or traced onto paper with a black pen, it is possible to lay the fabric over the drawing and trace the shape directly onto the fabric using a fabric pen or pencil. To make this easier, attach the drawing and fabric to a window with masking tape. Alternatively, cut out a paper template, lay it on top of the fabric and trace around the edge.

Mount the fabric in an embroidery frame as shown in Chapter 12 (*see* page 164).

Working method

Begin to couch the chosen thread along the centre line (A–B on Fig 3.3), turning it back on itself at

Fig 3.2
**Patterns for
couched and plaited rugs.**

Centre line

Small

Medium

Large

26

Couched Rugs

Materials

Almost any thread can be used for these rugs, for example, fine cord, string, chenille, wool, Perlé embroidery cotton, raffia or very narrow strips of fabric. Sewing cotton is used to stitch the main thread down. The amount required depends on the thickness of the thread used. For your guidance, the amounts used for the examples shown in Fig 3.1 were as follows:

Soft rayon cord, 3mm thick, required 4m (c. 4½yd)

Chenille, required 1½m (c. 1½yd) of the main colour and 1m (1yd) of the contrasting colour

Perlé cotton No. 3, required 3½m (c. 4yd.)

Size

As for selected pattern

the point given (B on Fig 3.3). Make two or three stitches very close to the beginning of the thread to hold the end securely and keep it from fraying. Continue to couch the remaining thread, working in a spiral and keeping each row close to the previous one (*see* Fig 3.3).

When the desired size is reached, remove the fabric from the frame and trim the edge to about 5mm (¼in). To turn the hem, fold this edge under and stitch it down. When turning the hem, take the end of the thread to the reverse side of the carpet, preferably on a curve, and secure with a few stitches. If the carpet is of cord or string, try to unravel the end on the reverse side before securing, so that it lies as flat as possible.

Press the carpet lightly on the reverse side with an iron or leave it under a book for a couple of days.

Fig 3.3 **Making up couched and plaited rugs.**

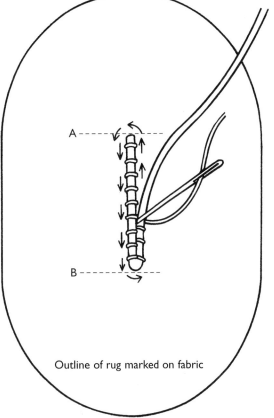

Outline of rug marked on fabric

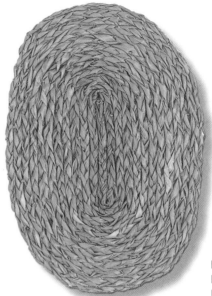

Fig 3.4 **Plaited rugs.
Left: stranded cotton.
Right: raffia.**

Plaited Rugs

Working method

Mark out the pattern on a piece of fabric as for the couched rugs (*see* page 26) and mount the fabric in an embroidery frame.

Plait the threads as shown in Fig 3.5, anchoring the starting point in a clamp or tied to a firm object. Take each outside colour into the centre alternately, then tie a knot at the finished end to prevent the plait unravelling.

Stitch the plait to the fabric in the same manner as for the couched rugs, but instead of taking the holding stitch right across the surface of the plait, stitch down through the plait, alternating from one side to the other (*see* Fig 3.6). This shows the plaited effect to greater advantage.

Finish the edge of the rugs as for the couched rugs (*see* page 27).

Fig 3.5 **Method
of plaiting.**

Fig 3.6 **Method
of stitching.**

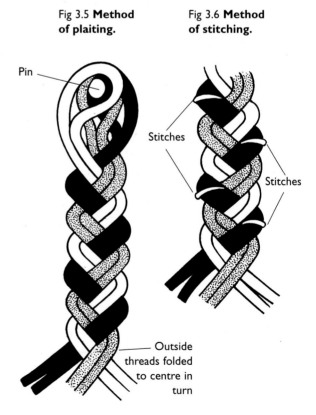

Pin

Stitches

Stitches

Outside
threads folded
to centre in
turn

Plaited Rugs

Materials

Suitable threads for a plaited rug include Perlé cotton, stranded cotton, raffia or fine wool. The rugs shown require a plaited length of 130cm (51in).

The raffia rug used three pieces of raffia, each 160cm (63in) long. If the raffia you are using is too wide, split and tear it down its length.

The stranded cotton rug used three pieces 320cm (126in) long, each of six strands. The cotton was folded in half and used double to give twelve strands.

Size

Both designs:

60 x 40mm (2⅜ x 1⁹⁄₁₆in)

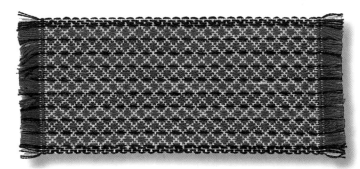

Fig 3.7 **Darned rugs. Top: diamond pattern. Bottom: basketweave pattern.**

Darned Rugs

Preparation

Mark the required size of the rug on the fabric with either a fabric pen or a tacking line, making sure the straight grain of the fabric runs along the length of the rug.

Working method

Begin the stitching by drawing the embroidery thread under two threads of the fabric and making a back stitch, as shown in Fig 3.8. Leave an end of about 25mm (1in).

Work along the row following the desired pattern and finish with another backstitch over

Fig 3.8 **Stitch patterns for darned rugs. Top: a simple basketweave effect. Bottom: a diamond pattern.**

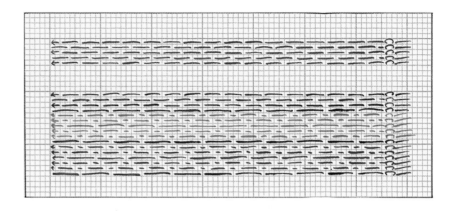

two threads, again leaving an end of about 25mm (1in). These ends form the fringe.

For a basketweave effect, darn over three threads and under one thread of the fabric to the end of the row. Alternate this pattern with each row so that the 'under one' lies in the centre of the 'over three' of the previous row.

For a diamond pattern, begin by working three rows of the basketweave pattern, as above, to form a border. Then, follow the stitch pattern in Fig 3.8, taking the embroidery thread over and

under the number of fabric threads as indicated.

Remember that every row begins and ends with a backstitch over two fabric threads, leaving an end to become part of the fringe.

Continue, row after row, until the desired width is reached, finishing with three rows of basketweave pattern. Trim the longer side edges of the fabric to 10mm (⅜in) and turn to the wrong side. Secure the edge neatly with a row of backstitch 5mm (³⁄₁₆in) from the edge, and then oversew the cut edge to prevent fraying.

Darned Rugs

Materials

These rugs are worked on an evenweave fabric as they are based on counted darning patterns. Two variations are shown, but it is very simple to invent your own. Be careful not to have any stitches longer than five threads as this will look out of scale.

The examples shown are worked on a 32 count evenweave linen, using three strands of stranded cotton and a No. 26 tapestry needle. Other counts can be used, for example, 18, 24 or 27, but you may need to increase the number of cotton strands in order to cover the fabric. Suitable threads include stranded cotton, flower thread and crewel wool.

Size

As required

Making the fringes

To make the fringed ends, cut across the ends of the rug, through both the fabric and the thread ends, between 5 and 10mm (³⁄₁₆ and ³⁄₈in) from the stitching, depending on the length of fringe wanted. Use the grain of the fabric as a guide to achieve a straight edge.

Finally, fray the fabric back to the end of the stitching and stroke the fringed ends together.

Fig 3.9 **A colourful rag rug.**

Rag Rugs

These very humble, utilitarian rugs were made from fabric scraps. They are suitable for servants' rooms or a small cottage.

Preparation

Mount the fabric in a tambour (a round frame) as shown in Chapter 12 (*see* page 166). Mark the required size on the muslin with a pencil or fabric pen. Appropriate sizes are 75 x 45mm

Rag Rugs

Materials

For a miniature rag rug to look in scale, the background fabric must be a fine muslin or scrim. Both are very loosely woven so they will accommodate the fabric strips.

For the strips, any closely-woven fabric is suitable, but fine, pure cotton or felt are best as they do not fray too much.

Use a large darning or tapestry needle to work the fabric threads.

Size

As required

(3 x 1¾in), 100 x 50mm (4 x 2in), or one of the smaller oval shapes given in Fig 3.2.

Working method

Cut various coloured fabrics into narrow strips 3–4mm (⅛–³⁄₁₆in) wide and about 100mm (4in) long, taking care to cut on the straight grain. A rotary cutter is excellent for this.

Working in rows from one end of the rug, pull the fabric thread through, leaving an end of about 4mm (³⁄₁₆in). Cut off and repeat as shown in Fig 3.10. Continue with this simple stitch, using various colours, until the whole shape is filled.

When complete, remove the rug from the frame and trim the edge of the muslin to about 10mm (⅜in). Paint the back of the rug with diluted fabric glue (half glue, half water). Only

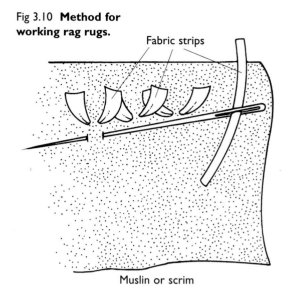

Fig 3.10 **Method for working rag rugs.**

Fabric strips

Muslin or scrim

a very light coating is needed. While the glue is still wet, turn the edges of the muslin under and allow the glue to hold them in position.

When the glue has dried, trim any longer tufts of fabric threads with sharp scissors.

Fig 3.11 **Canvaswork rugs. From top: Design B; Design A; Design C.**

Canvaswork Rugs

The three designs shown here represent different styles that appeared during the Victorian and Edwardian periods.

Design A, an all-over geometric pattern based on a design from the 1860s and early 1870s, is suitable for a mid-Victorian house.

Design B, with a scrolling stem of leaves and flowers, is based on one of William Morris'

Canvaswork Rugs

Materials	Size
For each design	**Design A**
Stranded cotton OR	62 x 30 stitches
Appletons crewel wool as listed in colour key	88 x 43mm (3½ x 1¾in)
Mono canvas (18 count): 150 x 100mm	**Design B**
(6 x 4in) or large enough to fit frame	54 x 29 stitches
Tapestry needle: No. 24	76 x 42mm (3 x 1⅝in)
	Design C
	69 x 34 stitches
	100 x 50mm (4 x 2in)

designs of 1878–80, which was produced at his Hammersmith works. This would suit a late Victorian house.

Design C, a symmetrical floral design within a decorative border, is also based on a Morris design. This one was produced at the Merton Abbey works during the very early twentieth century. The sample shown, with its dark blue background, would suit an Edwardian study or parlour. By substituting a lighter, perhaps cream background, it would look good in a bedroom.

Preparation

Mount the canvas in a small rectangular frame as shown in Chapter 12 (*see* page 165), and mark the edges with tacking stitches or a fabric pen.

Working method

Follow the relevant chart, using one strand of Appletons crewel wool or three strands of stranded cotton. Begin at the outer edge using tent stitch throughout. When the border is complete, work the central design from the central point. Remember, do not work the third row in from the edge until you are making up the carpet.

When the stitching is complete, block the rug if it has warped, as shown in Chapter 14 (*see* page 172).

Turn and complete the hem as shown in Chapter 2 and Fig 2.8. A fringe can be added if required (*see* pages 18 and 19).

Fig 3.12 **Chart for canvaswork rug, Design A.**

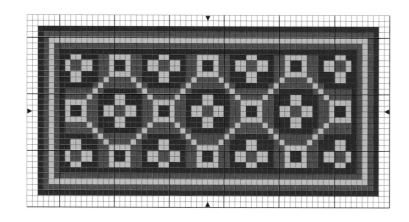

Fig 3.13 **Chart for canvaswork rug, Design B.**

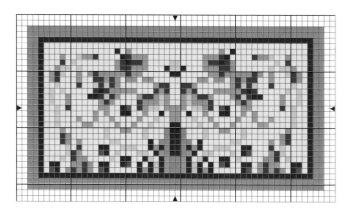

Fig 3.14 **Chart for canvaswork rug, Design C.**

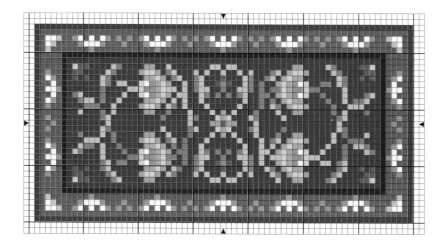

Canvaswork Rugs – Design A

		Skeins	DMC	Anchor	Madeira	Appletons
	Green	1	3348	253	1409	352
	Blue	1	312	148	1006	567
	Red	1	304	19	0510	995

Canvaswork Rugs – Design B

		Skeins	DMC	Anchor	Madeira	Appletons
	Dark green	1	935	862	1514	367
	Light green	1	3348	253	1409	352
	Dark turquoise	1	991	877	1704	527
	Light turquoise	1	993	208	1207	523
	Red	1	817	47	0509	502
	Rust	1	922	1003	0307	863
	Dark honey	1	3045	888	2108	902
	Light honey	1	3047	956	2109	692

Canvaswork Rugs – Design C

		Skeins	DMC	Anchor	Madeira	Appletons
	Dark green	1	935	862	1514	367
	Mid green	1	3346	262	1504	355
	Light green	1	3348	253	1409	352
	Dark blue	1	517	170	1107	566
	Light blue	1	519	1038	1105	563
	Dark rust	1	920	1004	0312	866
	Rust	1	922	1003	0307	863
	Dark peach	1	353	8	0304	862
	Light peach	1	945	367	2013	861
	Cream	1	712	275	0101	882

4 Curtains

At the end of the eighteenth century, the Empire Style was popular throughout Europe, spreading quickly from Paris where it began. In Britain it influenced the Regency Style of classically based, simple and elegant designs.

During the early nineteenth century, more importance was placed on curtains and draperies than in the previous centuries. Basic floor-length curtains designed to draw together were in common use. These generally had moulded or gilded poles ending with a finial or animal head.

Festoons and drapes continued to be used on only the very largest of windows. On such windows one, two or three drapes would be used, with or without end tails or tassels, and they would be topped by a carved, gilded or moulded curtain cornice instead of a pole or rod. The example in Fig 4.1 shows a full set of drapes, tails and tie-backs. This arrangement is suitable for the early Victorian period and for larger windows in upper class houses throughout the nineteenth century and the Edwardian period.

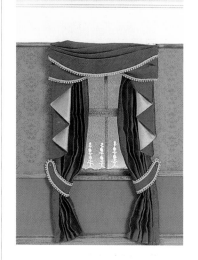

Fig 4.1 Curtains with a full set of drapes, tails and tie-backs.

Also in use were heavy outer curtains, which were not drawn, over either a pair of under curtains, which could be closed, or a painted blind.

Some plain curtains had richly embroidered borders with trimmings and fringes.

The early Victorian period, around 1840, saw a return to highly ornate curtain treatments, with deep drapes and large, ornate brass poles or pelmets. Outer curtains were fixed over lighter muslin or lace curtains, which were hung against the window. Also used were painted or printed roller blinds with fringed or openwork edges, and bed hangings were often matched with curtains.

As the century progressed, the styles in fashionable houses became increasingly heavy and ornate until, by the 1890s, almost every door, archway and window was hung with a portière (door curtain) or curtains dressed with drapes, festoons and tails, all further embellished with heavy fringes and tassels.

The exception to this was in households influenced by the Arts and Crafts movement. A popular movement from the 1870s to the 1890s, its influence brought a simpler style, typified by the use of 'homespun' fabrics with printed, woven or embroidered decoration. Curtains in this style were usually hung from a pole or given a simple valance or pelmet.

The Designs

Instructions for the various individual elements of curtain arrangements have been given, allowing a choice of combination. The following are guidelines for determining the correct positioning and size for curtains, or for adjusting curtains or patterns to fit any particular window or door.

Positioning and sizing

1 The hanging rail or top of a pelmet should be at least 10mm (⅜in) above the top of the window opening and should extend at least 10mm (⅜in) either side of the window opening (*see* A in Fig 4.2).

2 A full-length curtain is measured from the top of the rail or pelmet to the floor (*see* B in Fig 4.2).

3 A sill-length curtain is measured from the top of the rail or pelmet to 10 or 20mm (⅜ or ¾in) below the window opening (*see* C in Fig 4.2).

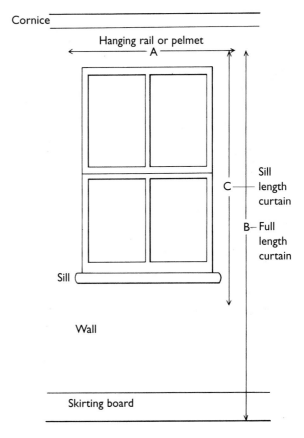

Fig 4.2 **Method of measuring the window to fit curtains.**

4 For the width of each curtain, as a general guide, the fabric should be cut at least three times the finished gathered width, with an additional 10mm (⅜in) at each side for turnings.

5 If the curtains are to hang from a rail or rod, a turning of 10mm (⅜in) is also required at the top and hem (*see* A in Fig 4.3). However, if a pelmet is to be used, the top hem allowance is not required (*see* B in Fig 4.3).

Fig 4.3 **Cutting diagrams for A: curtains to hang from a pole; and B: curtains for use with a pelmet.**

Top hem if using a rail or rod

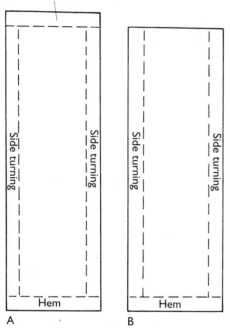

Curtains

Materials

The most suitable fabrics to use are light-weight cotton or silk, as natural fibres hold their pleats more easily than synthetic fibres. Avoid thick or textured fabrics as they will appear out of scale. (*See* page 52 for suitable materials for lace curtains.)

Size

As required

Working methods for pleating

There are three basic methods for pleating fabric:

- gathering by hand;
- using a home-made pleater; or
- using a commercial pleater.

The advantage of the first two methods is that the pleats can be slightly varied in size, giving a much more realistic effect.

With a commercial pleater, there is no flexibility in size, resulting in a rigid regularity of pleats. A further disadvantage is the high cost of the pleater itself. You may not be able to re-use your home-made pleater as many times as a commercial one, but it is very easy to make another.

The gathering method

1 Cut the fabric to the desired size, allowing for any turnings and hems.
2 Turn and stitch or glue the hem, together with the top hem if a rail and rings are to be used. If you are using glue, use it very sparingly.
3 Next, turn and stitch or glue the side turnings.
4 On the wrong side, mark a grid of dots with a soluble fabric pen or dressmakers' carbon. The vertical rows of dots must align and have about 20mm (¾in) between each dot. The dots can be placed slightly irregularly across the horizontal rows in order to vary the size of the pleats (*see* Fig 4.4).

Fig 4.4 **Marking a curtain for gathering.**

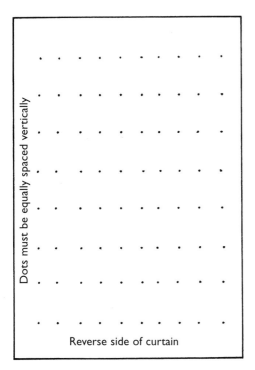

Dots must be equally spaced vertically

Reverse side of curtain

5 Thread a needle with polyester sewing cotton and fasten on securely with a double stitch. Pick up a little fabric with the needle at each dot, working along each of the horizontal rows. Leave

Fig 4.5 **Gathering method.**

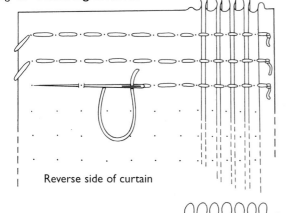

Reverse side of curtain

End view after gathering

the thread free at the end of each row (*see* Fig 4.5). Complete all rows before gathering up.

6 Draw up each individual row fairly tightly and fasten off the thread. As each row is completed, stroke a needle down the pleat to remove any wrinkles.

7 When all the rows have been drawn up, and using tongs to protect your fingers, hold the fabric in front of a steam iron and allow the steam to penetrate the pleats. (If you are using a synthetic fabric, you may need to press the iron lightly onto the fabric.)

8 Leave the curtain gathered up until it is completely dry. The longer you leave it the better.

9 Gently unfasten each end of the threads and remove them.

Home-made pleater

1 Cut a piece of 5mm (³⁄₁₆in) thick polystyrene foam or Foam-Cor 50mm (2in) wider and longer than the finished curtain. (Foam-Cor is composed of two thin sheets of card with a layer of high density foam sandwiched between them. It is available from art suppliers and is very easy to cut.)

2 With a sharp craft knife, cut parallel lines lengthways down the card at intervals of 3–5mm (⅛–³⁄₁₆in). Be careful not to cut right through the card or polystyrene.

3 Use the pleater in the same way as a commercial pleater (*see* instructions below), using two thin strips of acrylic sheet or two metal rulers to push the fabric into the slots.

Commercial pleater

A commercial pleater is a pliable plastic sheet with regular slots running down its length.

1 Turn any hems or side seams on the fabric.
2 Dampen the fabric slightly, and lay it over the pleater with the side edge of the curtain at one edge of the pleater. Using one of the two cards provided, push the fabric into the first slot (*see* Fig 4.6).

Fig 4.6 Using a pleater.

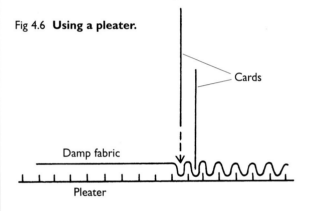

Cards

Damp fabric

Pleater

3 Leaving the first card in the slot, push the fabric into the second slot with the second card.
4 Leaving the second card in place, remove the first card and push the fabric into the third slot.
5 Continue in this way until the whole curtain has been fitted into the pleater.
6 Hold a steam iron over the pleater, without actually touching the curtain, and set with a jet of steam.
7 Bond a 20mm strip of Bond-a-web along the top edge of the curtain.
8 When it is completely dry, remove the curtain from the pleater by easing up the strip at the top of the curtain.

Working methods for pelmets

Basic pelmets

1 Four basic patterns for pelmets are given in Fig 4.7. Copy the desired pattern onto stiff card. The mounting card available in art supplies shops is ideal.
2 Cut out the complete shape with a sharp craft knife and metal ruler, then score gently along the inner lines to enable the card to fold sharply. Curves and shaped areas can be cut roughly and then finished off with sandpaper or an emery board. The length of the pelmet can be adjusted from the centre, and the lower front edge varied in shape if required.
3 If the pelmet is to be embroidered, the embroidery must be worked on the fabric before it is cut to cover the card so that the fabric is still large enough to fit into a frame.
4 To cover the card, cut the fabric for the pelmet at least 10mm (⅜in) larger all round than the card shape (*see* Fig 4.8) and apply a bonding agent, such as Bond-a-web, to the reverse of the fabric.
5 Lay a sheet of non-stick baking parchment on the work surface and, using an iron, bond the fabric to the front of the card. This will prevent the surplus fabric from sticking.
6 Fold the turnings over to the reverse side of the pelmet and gently bond into place, trimming or snipping into corners or shapes as you go to allow the turnings to press flat.

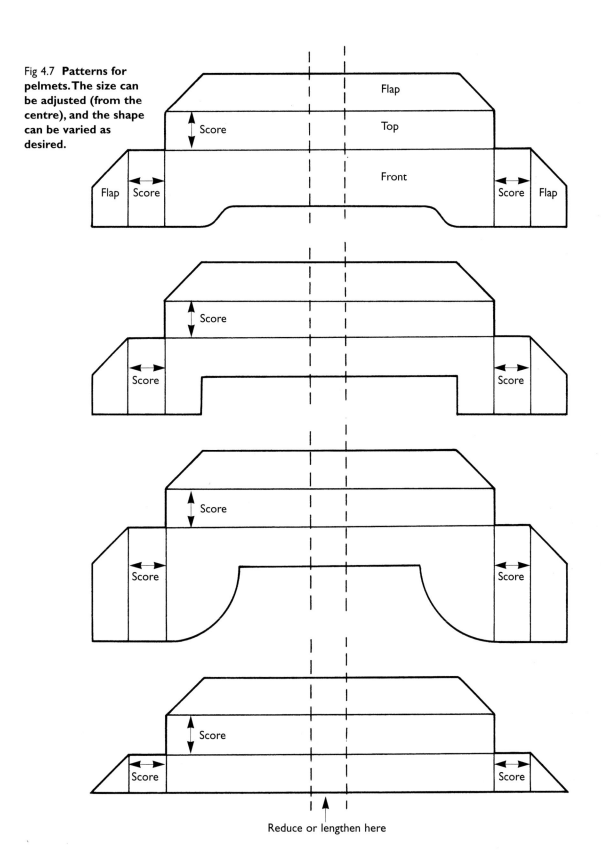

Fig 4.7 **Patterns for pelmets. The size can be adjusted (from the centre), and the shape can be varied as desired.**

Flap

Score | Top

Flap | Score | Front | Score | Flap

Score

Score | Score

Score

Score | Score

Score

Score | Score

Score

Score | Score

Reduce or lengthen here

Fig 4.8 **Covering the pelmets.**

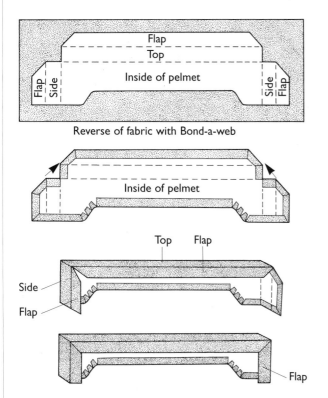

7 Add any braid or trimmings at this stage, using a little glue.

8 Fold back the sides and flaps along the scored lines.

9 When the curtains are ready and the pelmet decorated and covered, glue the top of the curtains to the inside of the pelmet front, then fold down the rear flaps of the pelmet and glue into position above the window.

Draped pelmets

The red curtains in Fig 4.1 are shown with a full set of drapes, tails and tie-backs. It is possible to select any combination to suit your needs – the full set, drapes without tails, a centre drape with tails, etc. If you are making drapes, you need to use the third pelmet pattern from Fig 4.7.

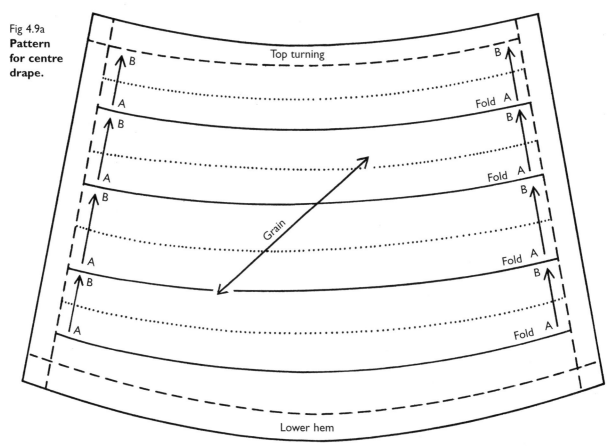

Fig 4.9a
Pattern for centre drape.

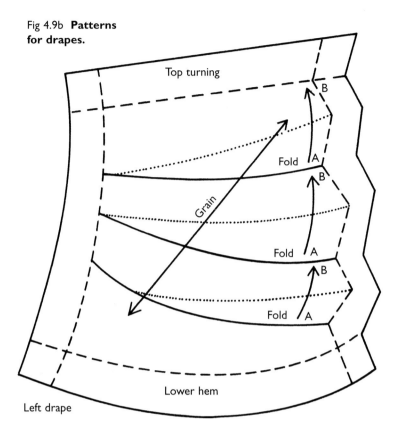

Fig 4.9b **Patterns for drapes.**

Top turning

B

Fold A

B

Grain

Fold A

B

Fold A

Lower hem

Left drape

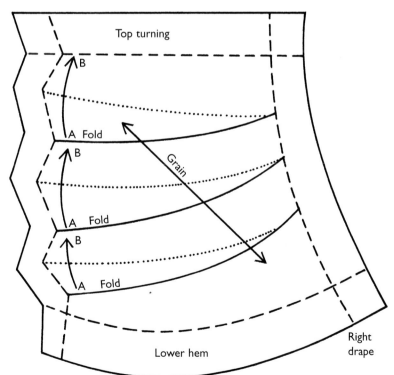

Top turning

B

A Fold

B

Grain

A Fold

B

A Fold

Lower hem

Right drape

1 Make and cover the pelmet as described above.

2 Trace off the patterns from Figs 4.9a and b. Cut one centre drape, one left- and one right-side drape. The fabric must be cut on the cross grain, as indicated in the patterns by the double-headed arrows.

3 Turn and secure the lower hems by sewing or gluing, and trim them with braid if desired. Use the fabric glue very sparingly.

4 Fold the pleats (indicated by the solid and dotted lines) so that **a** and **b** meet, and secure them with a small stitch to hold (*see* Figs 4.9a and b and 4.10A).

Fig 4.10 **Making up a draped pelmet.**

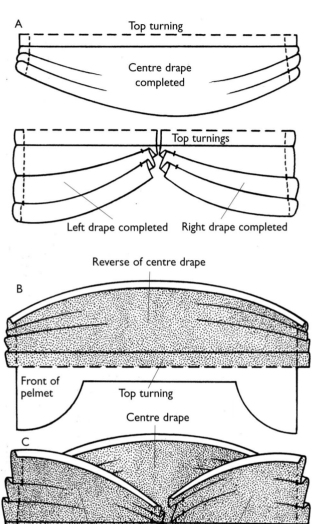

A

Top turning

Centre drape completed

Top turnings

Left drape completed   Right drape completed

Reverse of centre drape

B

Front of pelmet   Top turning

Centre drape

C

Front of pelmet   Top turnings

Reverse of left drape   Reverse of right drape

5 Hold the centre drape upside down and glue the turning to the top front edge of the pelmet, right sides together (*see* Fig 4.10B: reverse of fabric shaded).

6 In the same way, glue the top turnings of the side drapes behind the centre drape (*see* Fig 4.10C).

7 Turn the side edges of the drapes in and fold them down to the front of the pelmet. Glue the edges into place on the front of the pelmet (*see* Fig 4.12).

Tails

Working method

1 Select and trace the left and right tail patterns from Fig 4.11. Cut one of each, on the cross grain as indicated, in both fabric and lining.

2 Place each pair of fabric and lining pieces right sides together and stitch along three sides, as shown in Fig 4.12.

3 Turn through to the right side and press, then trim with braid if required.

4 Fold along the pleats as indicated on the pattern (solid and dotted lines on Fig 4.11), and press lightly with an iron, or leave under a book for softer pleats.

5 Glue the top edges of the tails into position inside each end of the pelmet (*see* Fig 4.12).

Tie-backs

Tie-backs, cords and tassels can all be used for holding back curtains. Instructions for tie-backs are given below, and instructions for tassels are given on page 46. Cords can be ready-made or lengths of thread can be plaited or twisted to produce a home-made cord.

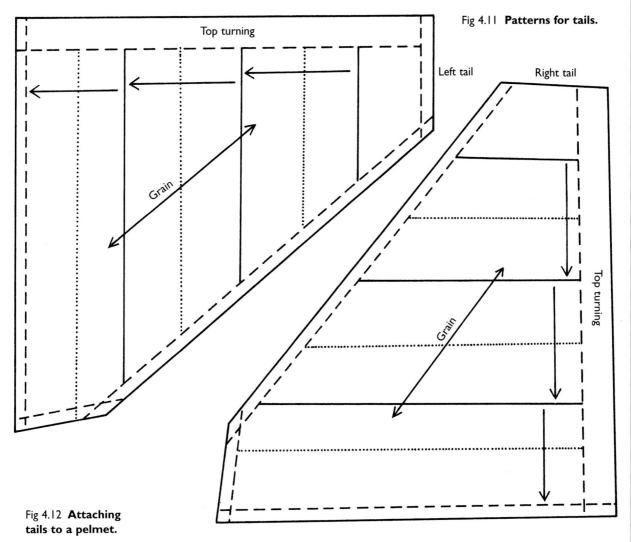

Fig 4.11 **Patterns for tails.**

Top turning

Left tail

Right tail

Grain

Grain

Top turning

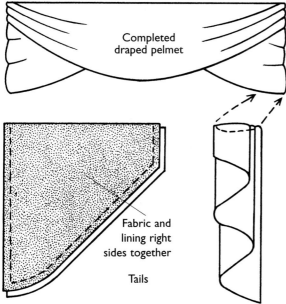

Fig 4.12 **Attaching tails to a pelmet.**

Completed draped pelmet

Fabric and lining right sides together

Tails

Working method

1 Cut a piece of fabric and one of lining, about 100mm (4in) square, and fix together with Bond-a-web.

2 Trace the pattern from Fig 4.13, making sure the tie-back is long enough to fold around your particular curtains. If it is not, lengthen the tie-back pattern from the centre.

3 Cut the bonded fabric to the exact size of the pattern – no turning is required.

4 Trim with braid, using either stitching or

Fig 4.13 **Pattern for tie-backs.**

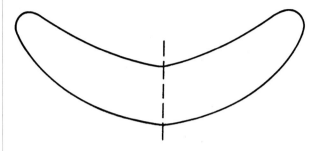

fabric glue. If you are using fabric glue, use it very sparingly.

5 To fit, make a small loop of braid or thread at each end of the tie-back, then fold it around the curtain and hook it onto a small pin which has been fixed to the wall.

OR

Thread a small bead onto a pin, fold the tie-back around the curtain and push the pin through the ends of the tie-back. Cut the pin down in length, leaving enough to fit into a small hole in the wall, and secure with a tiny spot of glue.

6 Gently arrange the curtain inside the tie-back to drape as desired.

Tassels

Working method

1 Cut a piece of stiff card into a rectangle 100 x 60mm (4 x 2⅜in), then cut a piece from the centre 50 x 30mm (2 x 1¼in). Mark the vertical centre line and cut a small notch in one side of the card to secure the thread. This size card will initially give a tassel that is longer than that required, but it is easier to handle.

2 Wind the thread around the card until the required thickness of tassel is achieved. Do not make the tassel too thick or the scale will be wrong.

3 Bind the middle 10–15mm (⅜–⅝in) of the tassel, using the centre line as a guide, then cut the threads at each end of the card.

4 Bend the tassel in half and bind the head to form a loop. Finally, trim the ends to the required length: probably 10–15mm (⅜–⅝in).

Fig 4.14 **Making tassels.**

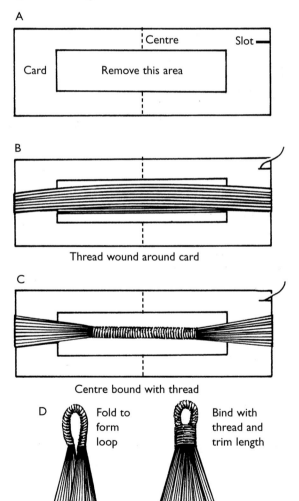

Fig 4.15 **Curtain settings with embroidered pelmets and side panels. These are suitable for a late Victorian or an Edwardian room.**

Embroidered designs

Preparation

If stitching a pelmet, select a plain pelmet pattern from Fig 4.7, but draw the pattern 15mm (⅝in) high instead of 10mm (⅜in). Tack an outline onto the fabric to show the size and shape of the pelmet or side panel (*see* page 38 for suitable fabrics), then draw the embroidery pattern in the centre of the pelmet or the lower section of a side panel, using dressmakers' carbon. (*See* Chapter 12, page 167, for methods of transferring designs.) Do not cut to shape yet as it is easier to work the embroidery in a frame on a larger piece of fabric.

Working method

Work the embroidery, following the chosen pattern (*see* Figs 4.16–4.19). The main stitch used for the designs in Fig 4.15 is backstitch, with detached chain stitch used inside the leaves of the Lily design. The scrolling design was worked in one thread of stranded cotton, in an old gold colour, and the Lily design in pale green (leaves) and dark cream (flowers).

For the design shown in Fig 4.20, one thread of stranded cotton was used throughout. The primroses were worked in pale yellow in detached chain stitch, with a French knot centre and buds of three chain stitches. The leaves were worked in mid-green backstitch.

47

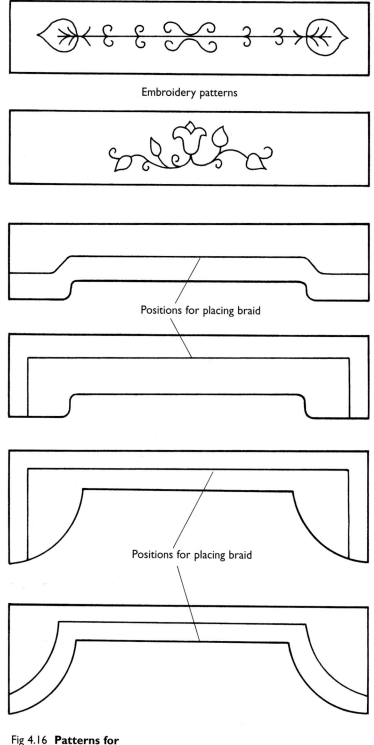

Embroidery patterns

Positions for placing braid

Positions for placing braid

Fig 4.16 **Patterns for
decorated pelmets
shown in Fig 4.15.**

Side panel

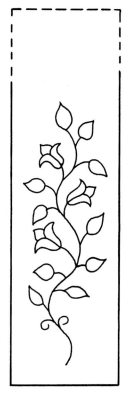

Side panel

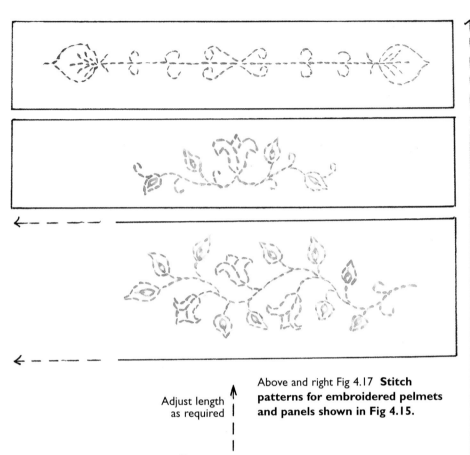

Above and right Fig 4.17 **Stitch patterns for embroidered pelmets and panels shown in Fig 4.15.**

Fig 4.18 **Pattern for Arts and Crafts movement curtains shown in Fig 4.20. Repeat the pattern as required to fill the length of the curtain.**

Adjust length as required

Centre edge of curtain

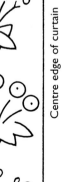

Adjust width as required

Fig 4.19 **Stitch patterns for Arts and Crafts movement curtains shown in Fig 4.20.**

49

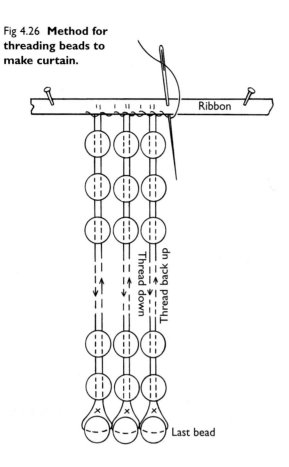

Fig 4.26 **Method for threading beads to make curtain.**

Ribbon

Thread down

Thread back up

Last bead

10 Place a pin in the board just above the last bead (indicated by x on Fig 4.26), and tighten the thread so that the beads touch. The pin will hold the row of beads in position whilst the next row is being worked.

11 Work two blanket stitches into the edge of the ribbon to complete the row. Make sure there is enough thread in the needle before beginning a new length of beads. To renew the thread, fasten off and on again into the ribbon.

12 Repeat each row of the chart, working two blanket stitches in between, until the curtain is complete, then fasten off securely into the ribbon.

13 Trim the ends from the ribbon and glue it to the back of a brass rod, a painted cocktail stick or painted dowelling.

14 Fit into position with glue or eyelets.

5 Cushions, chair seats & footstools

Embroidered cushions have been used throughout history to provide a degree of comfort and decoration. During the Victorian and Edwardian eras cushions were in everyday use, and were worked with great enthusiasm by the amateur embroiderers of the time.

The designs for the projects in this chapter have been adapted from nineteenth century examples and charts. A selection of patchwork and quilted designs, which were popular throughout the period, are included.

William Morris room setting.

Fig 5.1 **Canvaswork cushions. From left: Cat, Vase and Rose Spray designs.**

Canvaswork Cushions

Each design is shown with a selection of background colours, but any colour can be substituted provided it is a good contrast to the colours of the main design.

Preparation

Mount the canvas in a small frame (*see* Chapter 12, page 164) and mark the outer edge with a tacking line or fabric pen.

Working method

Follow the chosen chart, using two strands of stranded cotton if you are working on

Vase, Rose Spray and Cat Cushions

Materials	Size
For each cushion	**Each cushion**
Stranded cotton as listed in colour key	35 x 35 stitches
Coin net (24 count): 75mm (3in) square OR	38mm (1½in) square
Mono canvas (22 count): 75mm (3in) square	
Lightweight fabric for back of cushion (colour to tone with main colour of design)	
Filling material (*see* Filling cushions, page 80)	
Tapestry needle: No. 24 or 26	

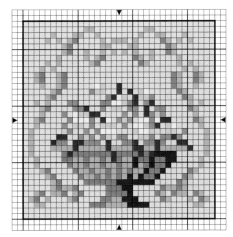

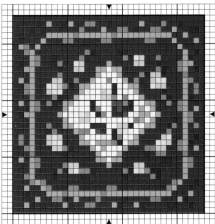

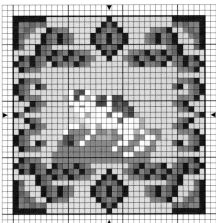

Far left Fig 5.2 **Chart for Rose Vase cushion (c. 1845).**

Left Fig 5.3 **Chart for Rose Spray cushion (late 1840s).**

Below left Fig 5.4 **Chart for Cat cushion (based on a hand-painted chart by L. W. Wittich of Berlin: 1850s).**

coin net or 22 count canvas, and three strands if you are working on 18 count canvas.

Using tent stitch, work the design first and then fill in the background.

If your embroidery has distorted the canvas, block it into shape on completion. (*See* Chapter 14, page 172.)

Make up the cushion as described on page 79, and finish the edges using one of the methods described on page 80.

Vase Cushion

		Skeins	DMC	Anchor	Madeira
	Gold	I	834	874	2206
	Tan	I	435	1046	2010
	Brown	I	801	359	2007
	Light pink	I	818	271	0608
	Dark pink	I	776	24	0607
	Mauve	I	3042	870	0807
	Light green	I	3053	260	1603
	Dark green	I	3051	268	1508

Alternative backgrounds

	Light blue	I	799	145	0910
	Grey (on chart)	I	453	231	1806

Rose Spray Cushion

		Skeins	DMC	Anchor	Madeira
	Gold	1	834	874	2206
	Light green	1	3053	260	1603
	Dark green	1	3051	268	1508
	Mauve	1	3042	870	0807
	Light pink	1	818	271	0608
	Dark pink	1	776	24	0607
	Light red	1	321	47	0510
	Dark red	1	815	43	0512
	Cream	1	677	886	2207

Alternative backgrounds

		Skeins	DMC	Anchor	Madeira
	Black	1	310	403	Black
	Dark red (on chart)	1	815	43	0512

Cat Cushion

		Skeins	DMC	Anchor	Madeira
	Gold	1	834	874	2206
	Tan	1	435	1046	2010
	Brown	1	801	359	2007
	Light rust	1	921	1003	0311
	Dark rust	1	355	1014	0401
	Light red	1	321	47	0510
	Dark red	1	815	43	0512
	Cream	1	677	886	2207
	Green	1	3053	260	1603
	White	1	Blanc	White	White

Alternative backgrounds

		Skeins	DMC	Anchor	Madeira
	Dark blue	1	797	147	0912
	Grey (on chart)	1	453	231	1806

Fig 5.5 **Canvaswork cushions: posy and garland designs.**

Floral Posy, Garland and Grisaille Cushions

Materials

For each cushion

Stranded cotton as listed in colour key

Coin net (24 count): 75mm (3in) square OR

Mono canvas (18 count): 75mm (3in) square

Lightweight fabric for back of cushion (colour to tone
with main colour of design)

Filling material (*see* Filling cushions, page 80)

Tapestry needle: No. 26 or 28

Size

Each cushion

29 x 29 stitches

30mm (1³⁄₁₆in) square on coin net OR

40mm (1⁹⁄₁₆in) square on mono canvas
(18 count)

Canvaswork Cushions – Floral Posy and Garland Cushions

		Skeins	DMC	Anchor	Madeira
	Dark pink	1	917	89	0706
	Purple	1	553	99	0711
	Red	1	321	47	0510
	Pale pink	1	894	26	0414
	Yellow	1	444	297	0105
	Light green	1	703	238	1307
	Bottle green	1	700	229	1305

Alternative backgrounds

	Dark red	1	815	43	0512
	Dark blue	1	820	134	0904
	Dark green (on chart)	1	319	683	1313

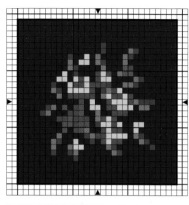
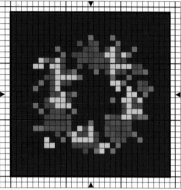

Fig 5.6 **Charts for Posy and Garland cushions (both c. 1860s).**

Fig 5.7 **Grisaille cushion.**

Canvaswork Cushions – Grisaille Cushion

		Skeins	DMC	Anchor	Madeira
	Dark grey	1	413	236	1713
	Medium grey	1	318	399	1802
	Pale grey	1	762	234	1804
	White	1	Blanc	White	White

Alternative backgrounds

	Blue (on chart)	1	798	137	0911
	Red	1	815	43	0512

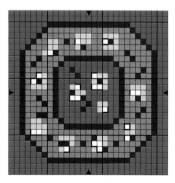

Fig 5.8 **Chart for Grisaille cushion (1850s–1860s).**

Embroidered William Morris Cushions

These projects are best worked on fine silk or cotton lawn fabric, but synthetics can be used if they are soft and pliable.

Flower Pot and Clanfield (designs introduced 1878–85) were originally designed for use as cushions or firescreens. Both were sold as finished items and as kits by Morris and Co. (*See* Fig 5.9.)

Fig 5.9 **William Morris cushions. Flower Pot and Clanfield designs.**

Embroidered William Morris Cushions

Materials
For each cushion
Stranded cotton as listed in colour key

Fabric for front and back of cushion: approx. 100 x 200mm (4 x 8in)

Filling material (*see* Filling cushions, page 80)

Embroidery or crewel needle: No. 10

Size
Each cushion
40mm (1%₆in) square

Preparation

Mark the outline of the cushion on one half of the fabric with a tacking line. Transfer the design (*see* Figs 5.10 and 5.11) to the centre of the marked area using a transfer pencil, dressmakers' carbon or the photocopy method, then mount the fabric in a frame or card mount (*see* Chapter 12, page 164).

Fig 5.10 **Pattern for Flower Pot cushion.**

Fig 5.11 **Pattern for Clanfield cushion.**

William Morris Cushions – Flowerpot Cushion		Skeins	DMC	Anchor	Madeira
	Light blue	1	827	9159	1014
	Mid blue	1	799	145	0910
	Dark blue	1	797	147	0912
	Light pink	1	224	893	0813
	Dark pink	1	223	895	0812
	Light green	1	3053	260	1603
	Dark green	1	3051	268	1508

Fig 5.12 **Stitch pattern for Flower Pot cushion.**

William Morris Cushions – Clanfield Cushion		Skeins	DMC	Anchor	Madeira
	Mid blue	1	799	145	0910
	Light green	1	3053	260	1603
	Dark green	1	3051	268	1508
	Light terracotta	1	758	882	0403
	Terracotta	1	407	914	2312

Fig 5.13 **Stitch pattern for Clanfield cushion.**

Working method

Using one strand of cotton throughout, work the design in backstitch and small straight stitches as indicated on the relevant stitch pattern (*see* Figs 5.12 and 5.13).

When the stitching is complete, make up and fill the cushion as described on pages 79 and 80.

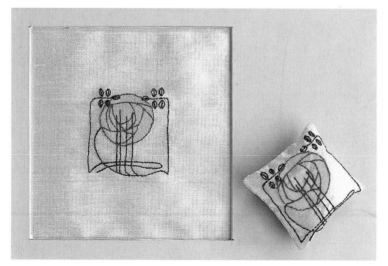

Fig 5.14 **Art Nouveau cushion.**

Art Nouveau Cushion

This pattern is based on *The Spirit of the Rose*, c.1900–5, designed by Francis Macdonald of the Glasgow School of Art. The original was worked in appliqué, satin stitch and couching.

Art Nouveau Cushion

Materials
Stranded cotton as listed in colour key

Fabric for front and back of cushion: approx. 100 x 200mm (4 x 8in)

Small piece of contrasting fabric

Filling material (*see* Filling cushions, page 80)

Embroidery or crewel needle: No. 10

Size
40mm (1⁹⁄₁₆in) square

Preparation

Mark the outline of the cushion on one half of the cushion fabric with a tacking line, then bond a small piece of the contrasting fabric to the cushion fabric where the circular part of the rose design will be positioned (*see* Chapter 13, page 170). Once this has been done, transfer the design (*see* Fig 5.15) to the centre of the marked area using a transfer pencil, dressmakers' carbon or the photocopy method, then mount the fabric in a frame or card mount (*see* Chapter 12, pages 165–168).

Working method

Using one strand of stranded cotton throughout, work the design in backstitch as indicated on the stitch pattern (*see* Fig 5.16).

When the stitching is complete, make up and fill the cushion as described on pages 79 and 80.

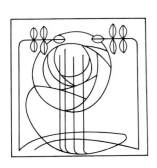

Fig 5.15 **Pattern for Art Nouveau cushion.**

William Morris Cushions – Art Nouveau Cushion		Skeins	DMC	Anchor	Madeira
	Red	1	816	1005	0512
	Green	1	937	268	1504

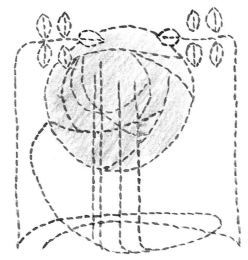

Fig 5.16 **Stitch pattern for Art Nouveau cushion.**

Edwardian Cushion

This design shows the very late Art Nouveau/Edwardian style. It is based on a small panel by K. Maud Mills, 1909, in the collection of the Victoria and Albert Museum, London. The original has applied velvet and silk embroidery on a blue silk background.

Fig 5.17 **Edwardian cushion.**

Edwardian Cushion

Materials

Stranded cotton as listed in colour key

Fabric for front and back of cushion: approx. 100 x 200mm (4 x 8in)

Filling material (*see* Filling cushions, page 80)

Embroidery or crewel needle: No. 10

Size

40mm (1⁹⁄₁₆in) square

William Morris cushions – Edwardian cushion		Skeins	DMC	Anchor	Madeira
▮	Dark green	I	3011	924	1607
▮	Light green	.I	734	280	1610
▮	Light grey green	I	504	1042	1701
▮	Gold	I	725	305	0106
▮	Pink	I	3326	36	0606
▮	Blue	I	799	145	0910

Preparation

Mark the outline of the cushion on one half of the fabric with a tacking line. Transfer the design (*see* Fig 5.18) to the centre of the marked area using a transfer pencil, dressmakers' carbon or the photocopy method, then mount the fabric in a frame or card mount (*see* Chapter 12, pages 165–168).

Left Fig 5.18 **Pattern for Edwardian cushion.**

Right Fig 5.19 **Stitch pattern for Edwardian cushion.**

Working method

Using one strand of stranded cotton through-out, work the design in backstitch, with small straight stitches for the 'feathers' and 'crests', and a small French knot for the eyes as indicated on the stitch pattern (*see* Fig 5.19).

When the stitching is complete, make up and fill the cushion as described on pages 79 and 80.

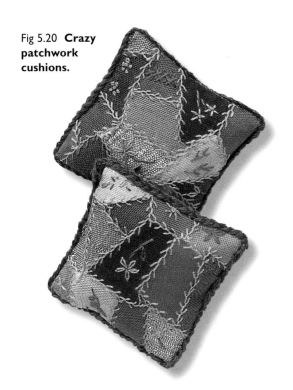

Fig 5.20 **Crazy patchwork cushions.**

Patchwork Cushions

Almost all the well-known patchwork patterns were popular throughout the Victorian and Edwardian eras. They were used in the lesser rooms of larger houses, and were in common use in modest houses.

The projects here include both real and simulated patchwork. It is most important to use only the lightest weight fabrics: pure silk and cotton are the best. Try to avoid synthetics for the methods using pieced patchwork as it is impossible to press the seams flat enough with synthetic fabrics.

Crazy Patchwork Cushion

Materials

A few stranded cotton embroidery threads in bright colours, including an old gold colour for main stitching

Fine cotton lawn or muslin: 100mm (4in) square

Bond-a-web (or similar): 50mm (2in) square

Selection of small scraps of coloured silk or fine cotton fabrics in bright, rich colours

Filling material (*see* Filling cushions, page 80)

Embroidery or crewel needle: No. 10

Size

30–40mm (1¼–1½in)

Fig 5.21 **Cutting and assembling fabric pieces for crazy patchwork.**

Crazy Patchwork Cushion

This method is technically closer to appliqué, as the scraps are laid on a fabric base. (*See* Chapter 9, page 123, for Crazy Patchwork Bedcover.)

Working method

1 Bond the square of Bond-a-web to the centre of the cotton lawn or muslin. Peel off the backing paper.

2 Draw the desired shape for the cushion on the bonded area. The square or circle can be from 30–40mm (1¼–1½in) as required. Cut the scraps of fabric into tiny irregularly shaped pieces, as shown in Fig 5.21.

3 Lay the pieces, mixing the colours, on the bonded area inside the outline. Allow each piece to overlap the next piece a little and press with an iron set to the right temperature for the fabric being used. This will fix the pieces to the backing, except for the overlapping edges.

4 Using one strand of the old gold cotton, work along the edges of the pieces with herringbone and feather stitches.

5 With one strand of the various colours of cotton, work small flower motifs in some of the shapes using backstitch, straight stitch, detached chain stitch and French knots.

6 Make up and edge the cushion as described on pages 79 and 80.

Fig 5.22 **Hexagon patchwork cushions.**

Hexagon Patchwork Cushion

This cushion uses a traditional hand-pieced patchwork method. (*See* Chapter 9, page 125, for Hexagon Patchwork Bedcover.)

Hexagon Patchwork Cushion

Materials

Tacking cotton

Fabric for cushion base: 75 x 150mm (3 x 6in)

Three different fabrics: 25mm (1in) squares
  (3 x fabric A; 3 x fabric B; 1 x fabric C)

Paper

Thin card

Filling material (*see* Filling cushions, page 80)

Embroidery, crewel or quilting needle: No. 10

Size

37mm (1½in) square

Working method

1 Trace the hexagon pattern from Fig 5.23A and cut out a template in thin card.

2 Using this card template, cut out seven paper hexagons.

3 Next, cut out hexagons from the seven fabric squares, 4mm (⅛in) larger all round than the paper templates (*see* Fig 5.23B).

4 Cover the paper hexagons with the fabric pieces. Fold each side over in turn and secure with a tacking stitch (*see* Figs 5.23C and D).

5 Assemble with fabric **c** in the centre and fabrics **a** and **b** alternating around the outside. To join the hexagons, place adjacent pieces right sides together and oversew the edges (*see* Fig 5.23E).

6 When all the pieces are joined, press well with an iron and remove the papers.

7 Cut the base fabric in half to form the front and back of the cushion, and mark the outline of the cushion with a tacking thread.

8 Lay the assembled motif in the centre of the

Fig 5.23 **Making hexagonal patches.**

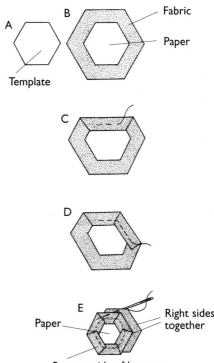

cushion front and stitch into position using small hemming stitches.

9 Press well.

10 Make up and edge the cushion as shown on pages 79 and 80.

Fig 5.24 **Simple nine-patch cushions.**

Block Patchwork Cushions

The secret of success when using this method of patchwork, is not to cut the fabric pieces too small. By allowing a generous turning, it is easier both to sew and to press the seams open. This may seem a waste of fabric, but it gives you more to hold on to and, ultimately, saves time. The excess seam allowance should be cut away after pressing.

As always for miniature work, a lightweight fabric – either silk or fine cotton – is necessary.

Use a sewing machine for the first seams which join the initial strips together. These strips are subsequently cut across their width, and the machine stitching will not unravel as hand stitching does. The remaining seams can then be stitched by hand with running stitches if preferred.

The following three blocks can also be used to make up a bedcover (*see* Chapter 9).

Nine-patch Cushion

Materials
For one block
Fabric A: 180 x 35mm (7 x 1½in)
Fabric B: 180 x 35mm (7 x 1½in)
Sewing thread, to match fabrics
Filling material (*see* Filling cushions, page 80)
Embroidery, crewel or quilting needle: No. 10

Size
32mm (1¼in) square

A Simple Nine-Patch Cushion

Working method

1 Cut two pieces from colour A of 40 x 18mm (1½ x ¾in) and one piece from colour B of 40 x 30mm (1½ x 1¼in).

2 Join the 40mm (1½in) edges together (*see* Fig 5.25A), allowing 6mm (¼in) for the seams.

3 Press the seams open with an iron and trim to 3mm (⅛in).

4 Cut in half across the stripes, (*see* Figs 5.25B and C).

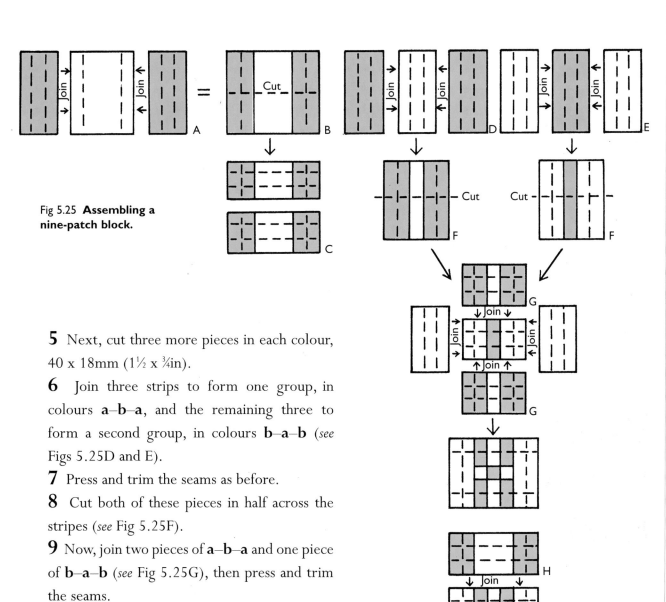

Fig 5.25 **Assembling a nine-patch block.**

5 Next, cut three more pieces in each colour, 40 x 18mm (1½ x ¾in).

6 Join three strips to form one group, in colours **a–b–a**, and the remaining three to form a second group, in colours **b–a–b** (*see* Figs 5.25D and E).

7 Press and trim the seams as before.

8 Cut both of these pieces in half across the stripes (*see* Fig 5.25F).

9 Now, join two pieces of **a–b–a** and one piece of **b–a–b** (*see* Fig 5.25G), then press and trim the seams.

10 Cut two final pieces of colour B, 30 x 18mm (1¼ x ¾in), and join one to each side of the piece formed above, then press and trim the seams.

11 Now join the two pieces formed in step 4 to the upper and lower edges of the main piece, formed in step 10 (*see* Fig 5.25H). Press and trim the seams. You now have one block with a 6mm (¼in) turning all round.

12 Make up and edge the cushion using one of the methods shown on pages 79 and 80.

Fig 5.26 **Little House on the Prairie cushions.**

Little House on the Prairie Cushion

Working method

1 Cut a strip of light blue, red, and light cream, each 50 x 25mm (2 x 1in).

2 Cut a strip of green and dark cream, each 40 x 25mm (1½ x 1in).

3 Allowing 6mm (¼in) for the seams, use a sewing machine to join the light blue strip to the red, and the red strip to the dark cream so that the red strip, in the centre, is 9mm (⅜in) wide (*see* Fig 5.27A).

4 Press the seam open with an iron and trim to 3mm (⅛in).

5 Lay this piece along a straight line and cut a strip at an angle of 45°, 18 x 30mm (¾ x 1¼in).

(*See* Figs 5.27B and C.) This forms the 'roof' section.

6 Now join the green strip to the light cream (*see* Figs 5.27D and E), then press and trim the turnings.

7 Cut a piece across the strip formed above, 18mm (¾in) long, and cut two pieces in light cream, both 18 x 25mm (¾ x 1in).

8 Join the three pieces together as shown in Fig 5.27F, making sure that the 'door' thus formed is 9mm (⅜in) high above the 6mm (¼in) seam allowance (*see* Fig 5.27G).

9 Press and trim the seam to 3mm (⅛in).

10 Cut one piece of dark blue and one of dark cream, each 30 x 15mm (1½ x ⅝in), and join together (*see* Figs 5.27H and I). Press and trim the seam as above.

Little House on the Prairie Cushion

Materials

For one block

Fabrics, light blue, red, green, dark blue: 50 x 30mm (2 x 1in) each

Fabrics, light cream, and dark cream: 150 x 30mm (6 x 1¼in) each

Sewing cotton, cream

Filling material (*see* Filling cushions, page 80)

Embroidery, crewel or quilting needle: No.10

Size

32mm (1¼in) square

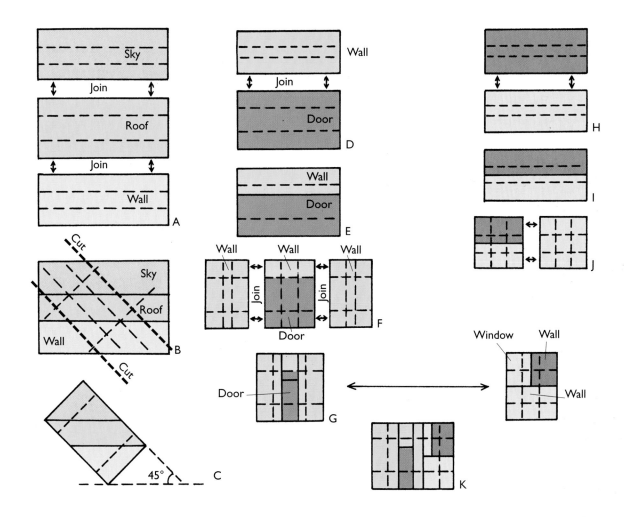

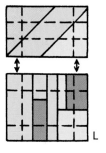

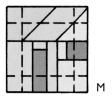

Fig 5.27 **Assembling a Little House on the Prairie block.**

11 Cut a piece across the strip, 18mm (¾in) long, and a piece of dark cream, 18mm (¾in) square. Join the two pieces as shown in Fig 5.27J, then press and trim as above. This forms the 'window' section.

12 Join the 'door' and 'window' pieces together (*see* Fig 5.27K), then press and trim the seams.

13 Join the 'roof' to the upper edge of the door and window piece, then press and trim. You now have the basic block with a 6mm (¼in) turning all round.

14 It is possible to add an outer strip by following the instructions given for the Nine Patch Cushion (*see also* Figs 5.25A–C and H).

15 Make up and edge the cushion following one of the methods given on pages 79 and 80.

Fig 5.28 **Log Cabin cushions.**

Log Cabin Cushion

Working method

1 Trace the pattern from Fig 5.29A onto the interlining. This will form the reverse side of the block and is the side from which the work is stitched.

2 Cut a piece of fabric for the centre of the block, and a piece for strip **a** in different colours, but both 12mm (½in) square.

3 Place both pieces in position on the *front* of the block, with the centre colour underneath (*see* Fig 5.29B).

4 Turn to the *reverse* side of the interlining piece and stitch along the line **x–x**, indicated on Fig 5.29C.

5 Trim the turning beside the stitching, fold strip **a** back and press with an iron (*see* Fig 5.29D).

6 Cut strip **b** in the same colour as **a**, and place in position on the right side of the interfacing as before. Turn the work to the reverse side and stitch along the line between the centre and strip **b**.

Log Cabin Cushion

Materials
For one block

Vilene sew-in interlining or similar (for base fabric): 100mm (4in) square

Fabric strips in five colours, 175 x 18mm (7 x ¾in) each

Sewing thread, to match fabrics

Filling material (*see* Filling cushions, page 80)

Quilting needle: No. 10 or 12

Size

32mm (1¼in) square

7 Trim back the turning and press as before (*see* Fig 5.29E).

8 Change colour to cut strips **c** and **d**, both 18mm (¾in), and stitch them to the interfacing in the same way as above (*see* Figs 5.29F and G).

9 Continue in this way, changing colour and increasing the length of the pieces for each round as below:

> Strips **e** and **f**: third colour, 25 x 20mm (1 x ¾in)
>
> Strips **g** and **h**: fourth colour, 30 x 20mm (1¼ x ¾in)
>
> Strips **i** and **j**: return to first colour (as for strips **a** and **b**), 25 x 20mm (1 x ¾in)
>
> Strips **k** and **l**: return to second colour (as for strips **c** and **d**), 30 x 20mm (1¼in x ¾in)

Remember to trim any excess turnings as you go and before pressing the pieces back on themselves.

10 When the block is complete, an additional outer round can be added to the cushion. Cut four strips in the centre colour, each 45 x 20mm (1¼ x ¾in), and stitch in the same way.

11 Make up and edge the cushion using one of the methods shown on pages 79 and 80.

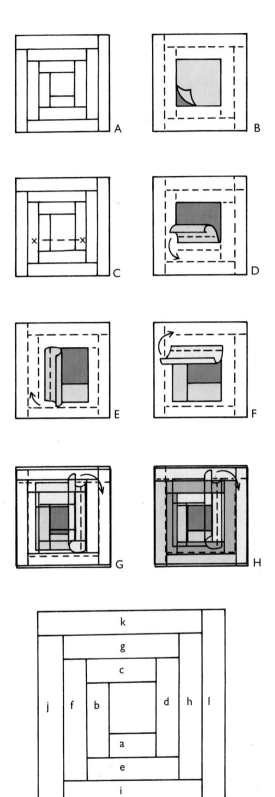

Fig 5.29 **Assembling a Log Cabin block.**

Fig 5.30 **Simulated patchwork cushions using striped fabric (left) and fabric transfer paints (right).**

Simulated Patchwork Cushions

Patchwork can be imitated in various ways, allowing some of the more intricate patterns to be reproduced to a true 1/12 scale.

Once you have completed your 'patchwork', make up and edge the cushions, to the size desired, as shown on pages 79 and 80.

Working methods for simulating patchwork

Striped fabric

The effect of a simple form of patchwork squares can be achieved through the use of striped fabric. The stripes must be of equal width.

1 Cut the fabric into strips about 20mm (¾in) wide, *across* the stripes.

2 Join the fabric strips, moving the fabric to align the stripes with a different colour. A fabric with several colours gives the best effect, but

Simulated Patchwork Cushions

Materials

Effective ways of simulating patchwork are through the use of striped fabrics, printed fabrics, fabric transfer paints and printed geometric designs, as described below.

Size

As required

even two colours works well.

3 Leaving a generous seam allowance to make handling easier – 6mm (¼in) – press each seam with an iron, then trim the seam to 3mm (⅛in).

Printed fabrics

Fabrics printed to imitate miniature patchwork are available. To give such fabric a slightly quilted effect and make the pieces look as though they have been stitched together (*see* Fig 9.13), follow the instructions below.

1 Lay the printed fabric over two or three layers of soft, fine muslin.
2 Using a No. 10 or 12 quilting needle, stitch along all the outlines of the pattern with tiny running stitch.

Fabric transfer paints

Any traditional patchwork pattern can be reproduced using fabric transfer paints. These paints are produced for use on synthetic fabrics and only give a subdued colour on natural fibres. Instructions for using them are given in Chapter 13 (*see* page 171).

Sheets of printed geometric patterns are available from art supplies shops and many of these are suitable for miniature patchwork. To give an idea of the size of pattern required to achieve the right scale, hexagons should have a diameter of about 6mm (¼in). You could also draw your own patterns, or reduce larger patterns on a photocopier. When the design is ready, on paper, follow the instructions below to create a patchwork effect.

1 Using fabric transfer paints, paint in the desired colours on the design.
2 Iron off the design onto the fabric (*see* Chapter 13, page 171).
3 Lightly quilt the fabric as described for using printed fabrics, above.

Fig 5.31 **Mock appliqué cushion.**

Mock Appliqué Cushions

True appliqué is too bulky to use for miniatures, but an effect which resembles appliqué can be achieved with bonded printed fabrics.

Working method

1 Iron a piece of Bond-a-web onto the reverse side of the printed fabrics.
2 Cut out some of the floral motifs and leaves, then peel the paper from the back.
3 Cut the background fabric in half for the front and back of the cushion.
4 Mark the required finished size on the cushion front with a tacking line.

Mock Appliqué Cushion

Materials

For one cushion

Background fabric: 200 x 100mm (8 x 4in)

Fabric scraps with small floral print

Fine, transparent chiffon: 200mm (8in) square

Bond-a-web or similar bonding agent

Filling material (*see* Filling cushions, page 80)

Quilting needle: No. 10 or 12

Size

As required

5 Arrange the motifs on the front of the cushion within the outline and press with an iron to bond them.

6 Lay the piece of fine chiffon over the cushion front and stitch around each motif with a tiny running stitch.

7 Make up and edge the cushion as shown on pages 79 and 80.

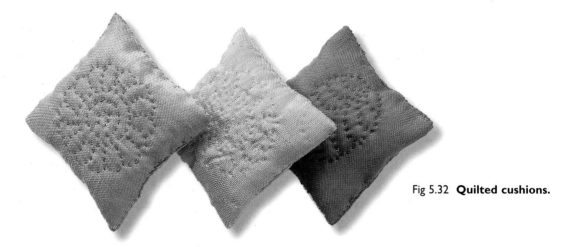

Fig 5.32 **Quilted cushions.**

Quilted Cushions

Quilted cushions were popular throughout the Victorian and Edwardian periods. Use only soft, lightweight fabrics such as silk, crepe, crepe-backed satin or fine cotton lawn.

Working method

1 Transfer the required design to the Habutai silk, using the photocopy method (*see* Chapter 12, page 168). A selection of the designs are given in Fig 5.33.

2 Press all the fabrics to be used to remove any creases.

3 Prepare for quilting by placing the Habutai face down with the four layers of muslin or the domette on top. Place the main fabric on top of this, face upwards (*see* Fig 5.34A).

4 Make sure the design is showing on the underside of the layered fabrics, then secure

Quilted Cushions

Materials

For one cushion

Fabric: 100mm (4in) square x 2

Light Habutai silk: 100mm (4in) square

Muslin: 100mm (4in) square x 4 OR

Domette: 100m (4in) square

Filling material (*see* Filling cushions, page 80)

Sewing or quilting thread to match fabric

Quilting needle: No. 10 or 12

Size

40mm (1½in) square

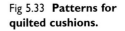

Fig 5.33 **Patterns for quilted cushions.**

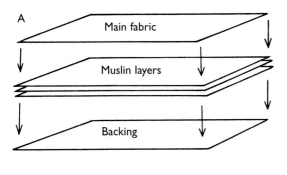

Fig 5.34 **Preparation of fabrics for quilting.**

with a loose tacking stitch to hold the sandwich together.

5 Working from the reverse side, with the Habutai silk and design showing, follow the lines of the design with tiny running stitches, beginning in the centre and working out to the edges. To start a thread, take it between the layers of fabric and bring the needle out at the point where the stitching is to commence, then make a tiny double stitch. Fasten off by making a tiny double stitch and running the end of the thread between the layers of fabric.

6 Continue until the whole design has been stitched.

7 Trim away the excess padding layer only, to the edge of the cushion (*see* Fig 5.34B).

8 Make up and edge the cushion as shown on pages 79 and 80.

Making up the cushions

1 Trim the seam allowances on the front and back of the cushion pieces to about 6mm (¼in), (*see* Fig 5.35A).

2 Turn the edges to the reverse side (*see* Fig

Fig. 5.35 **Making up cushions.**

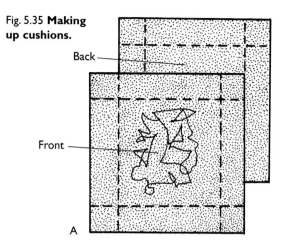

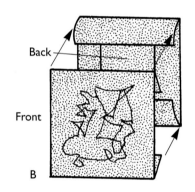

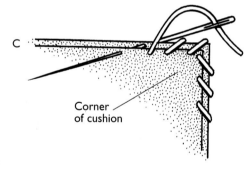

5.35B) and, using a No. 10 embroidery or quilting needle, stitch the two pieces together, beginning just before a corner (*see* Fig 5.35C).

3 Continue to stitch around three sides, finishing just after the final corner, thus leaving two-thirds of the remaining side open.

4 Fill the cushion (*see* below) and complete the stitching to close up the opening.

Filling cushions

If a firmly padded effect is required, fill the cushion with wadding or kapok. It is important to pull the wadding or kapok into the very smallest tufts, and to push these into the cushion working into the corners first. Do not be tempted to over-fill the cushion.

If you want a 'lived in' look, fill the cushion about three-quarters full with small beads. Plastic or glass beads are suitable, but they must be fairly small. This filling allows the cushion to be gently pushed into the corner of a chair, giving a very realistic effect.

Alternative edgings for cushions

The simplest method of working an edging on a cushion is to stitch around the edge with an oversewing stitch in a matching or contrasting thread. This gives a corded effect (*see* Fig 5.36A).

An alternative is to lay a couched thread along the seam of the cushion as shown in Fig 5.36B. Again, this can be stitched down with either a matching or a contrasting thread.

Using this method, a mock tassel can be created by leaving a loop of the laid thread at the corners. Wind the sewing thread around the loop two or three times and continue couching until the edging is completed. (*See* Fig 5.36C.) The loop can then be cut through and trimmed to give a tasselled effect.

Fig 5.36 **Alternative edgings for cushions.**

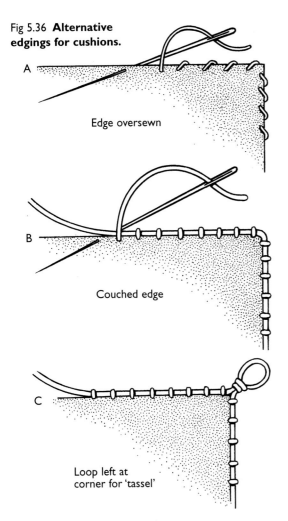

Edge oversewn

Couched edge

Loop left at corner for 'tassel'

Chair Seats

This selection of designs for chair seats can be used for ready-made chairs or kits.

If you are using a kit, there will probably be a pattern included for the size required, and this can be used to trace an outline onto the fabric or canvas.

For a ready-made chair, take a tracing of the size and shape of the seat, just inside the outer edge, and use this tracing to cut a template from thin card. This template can be used to trace the outline onto the fabric or canvas and also to mount the embroidery for the chair.

Working method for all chair seats

1 Using the template, mark the outline of the seat on the fabric or canvas with a fabric pen, then mark the centre line from front to back.

2 Work the chosen pattern from the centre line to one side, then move back to the centre again and work to the other side. Cover the shape of the seat with embroidery, working a little beyond the outline to allow for the padding of the seat – about two extra threads of canvas or four threads of fabric.

3 When the embroidery is complete, cut a piece of felt or very thin wadding slightly smaller than the card template (*see* Fig 5.37A).

Fig 5.37
Covering a chair seat.

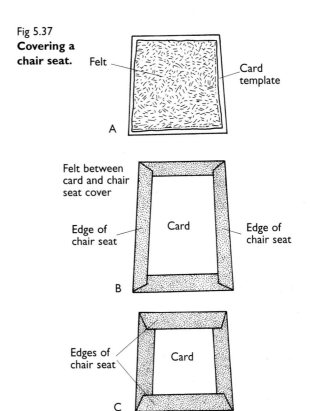

Felt

Card template

A

Felt between card and chair seat cover

Edge of chair seat

Card

Edge of chair seat

B

Edges of chair seat

Card

C

4 Position the felt (or wadding) on the template with the chair seat on top and, using PVA-based fabric glue sparingly, fold back and secure the two sides and then the front and back. Trim any excess fabric at the corners if necessary (*see* Fig 5.37B).

5 When dry, glue the completed seat to the chair with wood glue, taking care to centre it, so that a rim of the chair is showing all round.

Fig 5.38
Chair with a Florentine seat.

Florentine Chair Seats

This lovely technique, with its variations of pattern, was popular throughout the whole of the Victorian and Edwardian eras. It was worked in soft natural dyes until the late 1850s. This was followed with a trend for harsh chemical colours which stayed in vogue during the 1860s. From the 1870s, the fashion reverted back to very soft 'antique' colours.

When working full size, all the stitches for such designs are worked over an even number of threads – four or six. However, this does not give the right scale for miniature work, so the stitches are worked over three threads. The exception to this is on the 'medallion' patterns, where some stitches need to be over two or four threads to make the pattern correct. Also, when coming to the edge of the chair seat, stitches can be of whatever length is needed to finish on a line, as shown on the stitch patterns.

When choosing your colours, be careful that they are not too close or the contrast will not show up in the reduced scale.

Florentine Chair Seats

Materials

Stranded cotton in five toning shades (a good combination is three shades of one colour and two in contrast)

Tapestry needle: No. 28

For one chair

Linen evenweave (40 count): 100mm (4in) square

Card mount

For several chairs

Linen evenweave (40 count): sufficient to fit an embroidery frame, allowing 25mm (1in) between each seat shape

Embroidery frame

Size

As required: work to finished outline

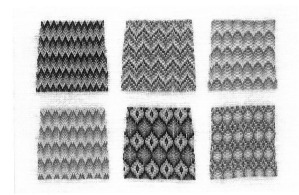

Fig 5.39 **Florentine seat covers.**

Working method

The patterns are worked with straight vertical stitches throughout, and adjoining stitches use the same hole.

With two threads of stranded cotton, work the stitches as indicated on the stitch patterns; most are over three threads and back under one.

Fig 5.40 **Stitch patterns for Florentine seats.**

Grisaille and Rectangular Garland Designs

The round and square Grisaille designs and the rectangular garland footstool, all shown in Fig 5.44, were worked on a 35 count evenweave linen, painted with fabric dye (*see* Chapter 13, page 171).

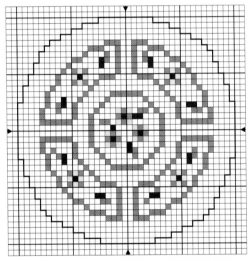

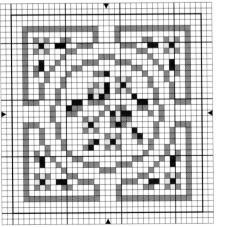

Left Fig 5.45 **Chart for round Grisaille footstool.**

Below left Fig 5.46 **Chart for square Grisaille footstool.**

Above Fig 5.44 **Grisaille and Garland footstools.**

Below Fig 5.47 **Chart for Garland footstool.**

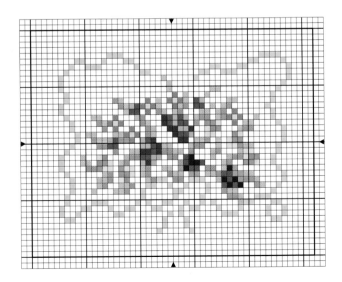

Grisaille and Rectangular Garland Footstools

Materials

Stranded cotton as listed in colour key

Tapestry needle: No. 26 or 28

Wood stain

Wood glue

Satin varnish

Card mount OR

Small embroidery frame

For each round footstool

Evenweave linen (35 count), painted with fabric dye: 100mm (4in) square

Button mould OR

Button with shank filed off: min. 22mm (⅞in) diameter

NB: It is possible to buy turned wooden bases, ready-made

Stripwood, obeche or jelutong: 2–3mm (⅛in) thick

Wooden beads x 3

For each rectangular and square footstool

Evenweave linen (35 count), painted with fabric dye: 125mm (4⅞in) square

Thin card

Felt

Stripwood, obeche or jelutong: 3–5mm (⅛–³⁄₁₆in) thick

Wooden beads x 4

Approximate sizes

Round footstool

25mm (1in) diameter

Square footstool

25mm (1in) square

Rectangular footstool

40 x 28mm

(1½in x 1⅛in)

Grisaille Footstools

		Skeins	DMC	Anchor	Madeira
	Pale grey	1	762	234	1804
	Mid grey	1	318	399	1802
	Dark grey	1	413	236	1713

Alternative backgrounds (if fabric not dyed)

	Blue	1	798	137	0911
	Red	1	815	43	0512
	Black	1	310	403	Black

Garland footstool (rectangular)

		Skeins	DMC	Anchor	Madeira
	Gold	I	725	305	0106
	Peach	I	352	9	0303
	Red	I	321	47	0510
	Dark red	I	815	43	0512
	Light mauve	I	554	96	0711
	Mid mauve	I	553	99	0712
	Dark mauve	I	550	102	0713
	Pale pink	I	776	24	0607
	Dark pink	I	602	63	0702
	Blue	I	807	168	1109
	Light green	I	472	264	1414
	Dark green	I	470	266	1410

Alternative backgrounds (if fabric not dyed)

		Skeins	DMC	Anchor	Madeira
	Cream	I	739	1009	2014
	Clover pink	I	224	893	0813
	Dark blue	I	824	132	1010
	Black	I	310	403	Black

William Morris and Art Nouveau Designs

The William Morris and Art Nouveau designs shown in Fig 5.48 were worked on a 35 count evenweave linen. The William Morris design is typical of his use of foliage. The Art Nouveau design is based on a fabric design by Harry Napper, c.1900.

Preparation

Mount the fabric into a card mount or small embroidery frame. Mark the outline and the centre of the desired footstool with a tacking line.

Fig 5.48 **William Morris and Art Nouveau footstools.**

William Morris and Art Nouveau Footstools

Materials

Stranded cotton as listed in colour key

Evenweave linen (40 count): 125mm (5in) square

Tapestry needle: No. 26 or 28

Wood stain

Wood glue

Satin varnish

Thin card

Felt

Stripwood, obeche or jelutong: 3–5mm (⅛–³⁄₁₆in) thick

Wooden beads x 4

Card mount OR

Small embroidery frame

Approximate size

40 x 28mm (1½ x 1⅛in)

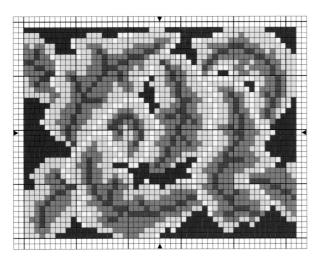

Fig 5.49 **Chart for William Morris footstool.**

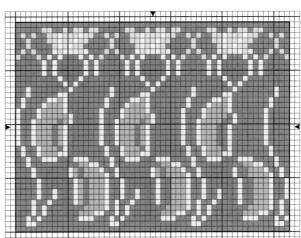

Fig 5.50 **Chart for Art Nouveau footstool.**

William Morris Footstool

		Skeins	DMC	Anchor	Madeira
■	Dark green	1	991	189	1204
▨	Mid green	1	502	876	1703
░	Light green	1	504	1042	1701
□	Cream	1	677	886	2207
■	Dark blue	1	820	134	0904

Art Nouveau Footstool

		Skeins	DMC	Anchor	Madeira
▨	Mid green	1	502	876	1703
░	Light green	1	504	1042	1701
▨	Dark peach	1	356	1013	0402
▨	Mid peach	1	758	882	0403
□	Light peach	1	957	50	0612

Making up the stools

Round designs

On completing the design, trim the fabric to shape, allowing a turning of 6mm (¼in) (*see* Fig 5.51B). With sewing cotton, stitch a gathering thread around the outer edge (*see* Fig 5.51C). Place the fabric over the button mould (or button), draw up the gathering thread and fasten off (*see* Fig 5.51D).

Draw a circle on the stripwood, slightly larger than the covered button mould, and cut it to shape. It is easier to cut the wood to a square first, then remove the corners to give an octagonal shape, and finally sand down the remaining points to produce a circle.

Glue three wooden beads to the underside of the base, using PVA wood glue, and when the

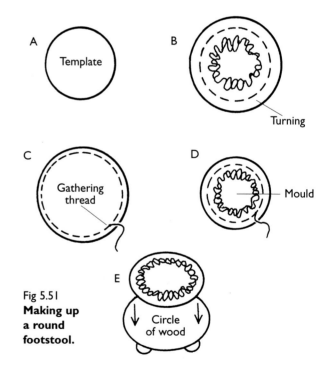

Fig 5.51
Making up a round footstool.

glue has dried, stain and varnish the rim and underside of the base as required. Finally, glue the covered button mould and base together (*see* Fig 5.51E).

Rectangular and square designs

On completing the design, trim the fabric to shape, allowing a turning of 6mm (¼in).

Cut a piece of thin card and a piece of stripwood to the required size of the footstool (*see* Fig 5.52A). This will be the same size as the completed embroidery.

Next, cut a piece of felt slightly smaller than the card and secure it with a spot of glue (*see* Fig 5.52B). Lay the embroidered fabric over the card to make sure that the embroidery covers the edges, unless a coloured fabric is being used. If necessary, trim the card until its edges are covered by the embroidery.

Using PVA glue, sparingly, fix the embroidered fabric to the padded card, securing the longer sides first. Allow these to dry, then secure the remaining sides (*see* Fig 5.52C).

Glue the beads to the underside of the base and, once the glue has dried, stain and varnish as required. Small cabriole legs are available commercially and can be used instead of beads (*see* Fig 5.52D).

The examples shown in Figs 5.43, 5.44 and 5.48 have been trimmed with bands of inlay for additional decoration. Such decorative bands are available from miniaturists' wood suppliers.

Finally, glue the covered card to the base (*see* Fig 5.52E).

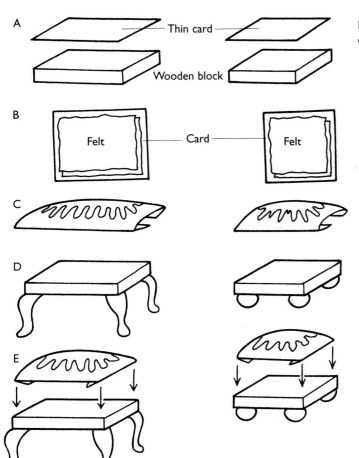

A — Thin card —

Wooden block

B Felt — Card — Felt

C

D

E

Fig 5.52 **Making up a square or rectangular footstool.**

6 Screens

Screens were used throughout the Victorian and Edwardian eras for a variety of purposes.

Pole screens, small, decorative screens which could be raised or lowered on a support, were placed near the fireplace. Their function was to protect a lady's complexion from the heat of the fire, hence the need for adjustable height. The decorative area of these screens – painted panel, needlework or woven tapestry – could be rigid and framed or alternatively, be in the form of a small banner hanging from a decorative horizontal pole. Such banners would have a fringe or tassels at the lower edge.

Fire screens stood in the fireplace to provide decoration when the hearth was not in use, and folding screens of two, three or four panels were used to provide privacy or to stop draughts.

The designs used for these items covered the full range of flowers, birds, and pictorial or narrative scenes that were popular throughout the Victorian and Edwardian eras.

The first three of the following designs could be equally well used for pictures. The patterns given for the embroidered screen panels would also make good wall hangings, and could be enlarged to create ornate window or bed curtains.

A folding screen.

Fig 6.1 **Oval Posy pole screen and three-fold screen.**

Oval Posy Screen

The Oval Posy design shown in Fig 6.1 is based on a piece (1840–1860) in the collection of the Embroiderers' Guild, which shows a floral posy within an oval.

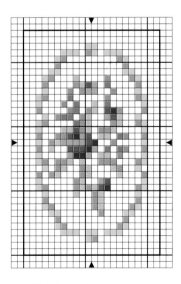

Fig 6.2 **Chart for Oval Posy screen.**

Oval Posy Screen

		Skeins	DMC	Anchor	Madeira
	Gold	1	725	305	0106
	Dark gold	1	680	907	2210
	Dark green	1	470	266	1410
	Light green	1	472	264	1414
	Pink	1	352	9	0303
	Red	1	666	9046	0210
	Dark red	1	815	43	0512
	Blue	1	799	145	0910
	Grey green	1	502	876	1703

Background (if canvas used)

	Dark cream	1	3047	886	2205

Oval Posy Screen

Materials

Stranded cotton as indicated in colour key

For pole screen

Evenweave linen (40 count): 100mm (4in) square

Tapestry needle: No. 28

Card mount OR

Small embroidery frame

Ready-made pole screen OR

Pole screen kit OR

Daler mounting board: 100mm (4in) square

Stripwood, obeche or jelutong: 2–3mm (⅛in) thick, 50mm (2in) square

Turned baluster

Wooden beads x 3

Small picture frame moulding

For folding screen

Mono canvas (18 count): 200 x 100mm (8in x 4in)

Tapestry needle: No. 26

Stripwood, obeche or jelutong: 3 x 45 x 133mm (⅛ x 1¾ x 5¼in) x 3

Stripwood: 2 x 6 x 1,250mm (¹⁄₁₆ x ¼ x 50in)

Thin leather, suede or vilene: 200 x 150mm (8 x 6in)

Sizes

Pole screen

29 x 19mm (1⅛ x ¾in)

Folding screen panels

each 50 x 32mm (2 x 1¼in)

Peacock Screen

The design for the Peacock Screen in Fig 6.3 is from a panel (c. 1850) in the collection of the Rochester Museum.

Fig 6.3 **Peacock pole screen and fire screen.**

Peacock Screen

Materials

Stranded cotton as indicated in
  colour key

For pole screen

Evenweave linen (40 count):
  100mm (4in) square
Tapestry needle: No. 28
Card mount OR
Small embroidery frame
Ready-made pole screen OR
Pole screen kit OR
Daler mounting board:
  100mm (4in) square
Stripwood, obeche or jelutong:
  2–3mm (⅛in) thick, 50mm
  (2in) square

Turned baluster
Wooden beads x 3
Small picture frame moulding

For fire screen

Mono canvas (18 count):
  100mm (4in) square
Card mount
Tapestry needle: No. 26
Daler mounting board:
  100mm (4in) square
Wood blocks: 15 x 5 x 5mm
  (⅝ x ³⁄₁₆ x ³⁄₁₆in) x 2
Small picture frame moulding

Sizes

Pole screen

32mm (1¼in) square

Fire screen

50 x 52mm (2 x 2¹⁄₁₆in)

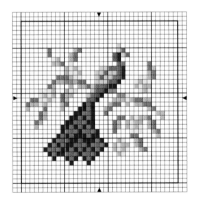

Fig 6.4 **Chart for
Peacock screen.**

Peacock Screen

		Skeins	DMC	Anchor	Madeira
	Dark blue	1	820	134	0904
	Turquoise	1	958	187	1114
	Bright green	1	996	433	1103
	Light pink	1	818	271	0608
	Dark pink	1	899	66	0609
	Gold	1	725	305	0106
	Light green	1	472	264	1414
	Dark green	1	470	266	1410
	Dark gold	1	680	907	2210

Background (if canvas used)

		Skeins	DMC	Anchor	Madeira
	Ecru	1	Ecru	926	Ecru

Fig 6.5 **Geometric pole screen and fire screen.**

Geometric Screen

The Geometric design in Fig 6.5 is typical of the 1870s.

Preparation for all screens

If you are working with a ready-made screen or a kit, measure the size of the embroidered area carefully and use this measurement instead of the sizes quoted above. If the screen itself is oval or round, trace around it onto paper to use as a pattern.

Mark the outside edge and centre lines of the design on the fabric or canvas with small tacking stitches.

Working method for all screens

Use tent stitch throughout, with one strand of stranded cotton on linen and three strands on canvas.

Select the required chart and begin working the design from the centre, removing the tacking stitches when they obstruct. If you are working on canvas, stitch the design first and then fill in the background. When working on linen the background is not worked.

Work one complete design for each of the screens except the Oval Posy Folding Screen, which requires three.

If the fabric or canvas has distorted, you may need to block it back into shape (see Chapter 14, page 172). Do this before trimming the excess turning from around the edges.

Making up the screens

Pole screens

If you are using a kit, follow the instructions provided by the manufacturer. If not, follow the instructions below.

Trace off the pattern for the base from Fig 6.7

Geometric Screen

Materials

Stranded cotton as indicated in
colour key

For pole screen

Evenweave linen (40 count):
100mm (4in) square

Tapestry needle: No. 28

Card mount OR

Small embroidery frame

Ready-made pole screen OR

Pole screen kit OR

Daler mounting board:
100mm (4in) square

Stripwood, obeche or jelutong:
2–3mm (⅛in) thick, 50mm
(2in) square

Turned baluster

Wooden beads x 3

Small picture frame moulding

For fire screen

Mono canvas (18 count):
100mm (4in) square

Card mount

Tapestry needle: No. 26

Daler mounting board:
100mm (4in) square

Wood blocks: 15 x 5 x 5mm
(⅝ x ³⁄₁₆ x ³⁄₁₆in) x 2

Small picture frame moulding

Sizes

Pole screen

32 x 27mm (1¼ x 1¹⁄₁₆in)

Fire screen

52 x 60mm (2¹⁄₁₆ x 2⅜in)

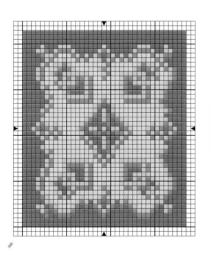

Fig 6.6 **Chart for
Geometric screen.**

Geometric Screen

		Skeins	DMC	Anchor	Madeira
	Gold	I	725	305	0106
	Dark gold	I	680	907	2210
	Dark green	I	502	876	1703
	Light green	I	504	1042	1701

onto the piece of stripwood, cut it to shape with a craft knife and trim or sandpaper the three corners away as indicated.

Drill a small hole in the centre of the base, with a diameter the same as that of the baluster. Glue three wooden beads under the base for feet, then glue the baluster into the hole. When the glue has dried, stain and varnish as required.

Next, take the piece of daler board, white side uppermost, and spread a thin, smooth layer of PVA fabric glue over the surface. Almost wipe the glue off as only the thinnest layer is needed: too

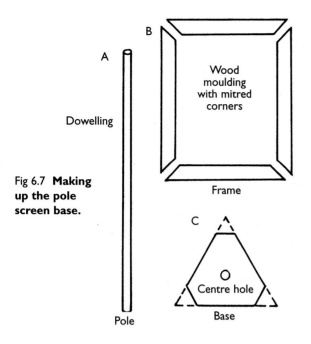

Fig 6.7 Making up the pole screen base.

Fire screens

Make the frame and mount the embroidery following the instructions for making up a pole screen. Sandpaper down the two little blocks of stripwood to take the upper corners off (*see* side view in Fig 6.8) then stain all the wooden pieces.

Glue the two blocks, with the length running from front to back, onto the bottom edge of the frame as indicated by the arrows in Fig 6.8.

Folding screens

Instructions for making up folding screens are given on pages 106 and 107.

Fig 6.8 Making up the frame for the pole screen and fire screen.

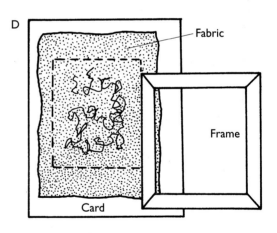

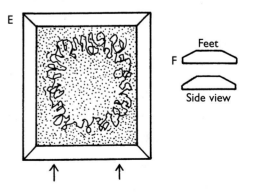

much will seep through the fabric.

Gently smooth the embroidered fabric or canvas into position in the centre of the card (*see* Fig 6.8), making sure that it is straight and squared. Leave it to dry completely.

Make the frame with a miniature moulding. The inside measurement should be the same as the outside finished edge of the embroidery. Mitre the corners of the frame and, using wood glue sparingly, secure the corners. Wipe away any excess glue immediately.

Once the glue has dried, stain and varnish if necessary.

Now glue the frame into position over the embroidery and card. Allow it to dry completely and then, with a very sharp craft knife, cut around the outside edge of the frame, through all the layers. Angle the knife inwards slightly to avoid the card protruding at the edges.

Glue the framed embroidery into position on the stand at the required height.

Embroidered Screens

The designs presented here could be enlarged to make curtains or wall hangings. They have both been worked on silk, but a lightweight cotton would also be suitable.

Fig 6.9 **William Morris-style screen.**

William Morris-Style Screen

This William Morris-style Screen is based on a design by J. H. Dearle, Morris' chief designer. The original screens were produced and sold by Morris and Co. (c. 1890). An example can be found in the collection of the Victoria and Albert Museum in London.

Preparation

Press the fabric to remove any creases. Transfer the design in Fig 6.10 onto the fabric by either tracing through the fabric with a fabric pencil or by ironing off a photocopy. Using the photocopy method will reverse the design. (*See* Chapter 12 for details of these methods.) Leave about 25mm (1in) between the designs for making up the screen.

William Morris-style Screen

Materials

Stranded cotton as listed in colour
    key
Lightweight silk OR
Lightweight cotton: 250 x 200mm
    (10 x 8in)
Embroidery or crewel needle: No. 10
PVA glue
Stripwood, obeche or jelutong: 2 x
    50 x 133mm ($\frac{1}{16}$ x 2 x 5$\frac{1}{4}$in) x 3

Stripwood: 2 x 5 x 1,250mm
    ($\frac{1}{16}$ x $\frac{3}{16}$ x 50in)
Wood stain
Wood glue
Satin varnish
Thin leather, suede or vilene:
    200 x 150mm (8 x 6in)
Small, rectangular frame

Size

Each panel
50 x 133mm
    (2 x 5$\frac{1}{4}$in)

Fig 6.10 **Pattern for William Morris-style screen.**

Fig 6.11 **Stitch pattern for William Morris-style screen.**

William Morris-Style Screen

		Skeins	DMC	Anchor	Madeira
	Light green	I	3348	254	1604
	Dark green	I	3011	924	1607
	Light grey green	I	504	1042	1701
	Dark grey green	I	502	876	1703
	Apricot	I	951	880	2308
	Light peach	I	353	868	0304
	Dark peach	I	352	9	0303
	Yellow	I	676	891	2208
	Red	I	815	43	0512
	Tan	I	435	1046	2010

Mount the marked fabric into a small, rectangular frame.

Working method

Use one strand of cotton throughout and refer to Fig 6.11 for the placement of colours.

Panel A is worked entirely in backstitch. For Panel B, work the flowers in satin stitch, the berries in French knots and the remainder in backstitch. For Panel C, yellow straight stitches are used within the petals, with green, pink and red seeding stitch used to fill the centre of the flowers. The remainder is worked in backstitch.

To make up the screen, follow the instructions given on pages 106 and 107.

Fig 6.12 **Art Nouveau/ Edwardian screen.**

Art Nouveau/ Edwardian Screen

This screen, which would suit both the Edwardian and Art Nouveau periods, has a design which is based on a hanging worked by the Royal School of Art Needlework (c. 1905), which can be found in the Victoria and Albert Museum in London.

Preparation

Press the fabric to remove any creases. Transfer the design from Fig 6.13 to the fabric by either tracing through the fabric with a fabric pencil or

Art Nouveau/Edwardian Screen

Materials	Stripwood:	Size
Stranded cotton as listed in colour key	2 x 5 x 1,250mm (¹⁄₁₆ x ³⁄₁₆ x 50in)	**Each panel**
Lightweight silk OR		50 x 133mm
Lightweight cotton: 250 x 200mm (10 x 8in)	Wood stain	(2 x 5¼in)
Embroidery or crewel needle: No. 10	Wood glue	
PVA glue	Satin varnish	
Stripwood, obeche or jelutong:	Thin leather, suede or vilene:	
2 x 50 x 133mm (¹⁄₁₆ x 2 x 5¼in) x 3	200 x 150mm (8 x 6in)	
	Small, rectangular frame	

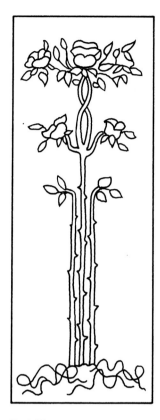

Fig 6.13
Pattern for Art Nouveau/Edwardian screen.

Art Nouveau/Edwardian Screen

		Skeins	DMC	Anchor	Madeira
	Light green	I	3348	254	1604
	Dark green	I	3011	924	1607
	Light peach	I	353	868	0304
	Dark peach	I	352	9	0303
	Apricot	I	951	880	2308
	Lemon	I	745	300	0111
	Light pink	I	3326	36	0606
	Dark pink	I	223	895	0812
	Terracotta	I	356	1013	0402

by ironing off a photocopy. The photocopy method will reverse the design. (*See* Chapter 12 for details of these methods.)

The pattern is repeated three times in the completed screen. Leave about 25mm (1in) between the panels for making up the screen.

Mount the marked fabric in a small, rectangular frame.

Working method

Use one strand of cotton throughout. Each panel of this screen has different coloured roses. The colour combinations are: light and dark peach; lemon and apricot; and light and dark pink. Refer to Fig 6.14 for the placement of colours. The roses and leaves are all worked in satin stitch and the remainder is worked in backstitch.

To make up the screen, follow the instructions given on pages 106 and 107.

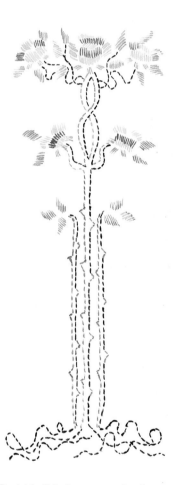

Fig 6.14 **Stitch pattern for Art Nouveau/Edwardian screen.**

105

Making up a three-fold screen

1 Cut the three pieces of stripwood for the backing to size – 50 x 133mm (2 x 5¼in) for William the Morris-style and Art Nouveau/Edwardian designs; 45 x 133mm (1¾ x 5¼in) for the Oval Posy Screen.

2 Sandpaper all the surfaces smooth.

3 Stain and varnish the edges and lower section of each piece where it will not be covered with embroidery. This is only the lower section for the William Morris and Art Nouveau designs, but almost half the length for the Oval Posy Screen. (*See* Fig 6.15A.)

4 Stain and varnish the 5mm (¼in) stripwood, and leave to dry.

5 Coat the area of wood on the backing pieces which will be covered by the embroidered fabric with a thin smooth layer of PVA wood glue. Allow the glue to dry completely.

6 Lay the embroidered panel in position over the glued area and, with a warm iron, seal one of the long sides of the fabric to the wood. This will adhere the fabric to the wood without marking it. Next, seal the side opposite, stretching the fabric slightly to avoid wrinkles.

7 Repeat this process with the top and lower edges.

8 Trim the excess fabric away from all four edges with small, sharp scissors. (*See* Fig 6.15C.)

9 Cut two long pieces of 5mm (¼in) stripwood and, using wood glue very sparingly, secure them along each side of the screen panel.

10 Cut three shorter pieces of 5mm (¼in) stripwood to fit between the sides and glue them into position as shown. This will cover the raw lower edge of the fabric (*see* Figs 6.15B and D).

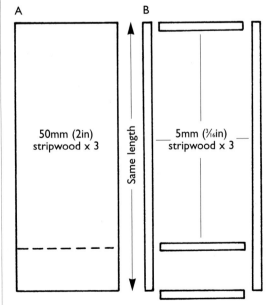
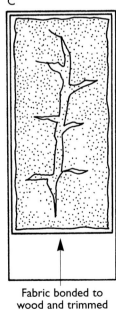
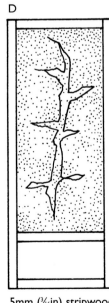

A

50mm (2in) stripwood x 3

Same length

B

5mm (³⁄₁₆in) stripwood x 3

C

Fabric bonded to wood and trimmed

D

5mm (³⁄₁₆in) stripwood glued into position

Fig 6.15 **Making up panels for the three-fold screen.**

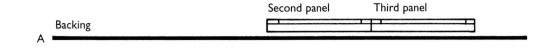

Second panel   Third panel

Backing

A

Fig 6.16 **Assembling
the panels for the
three-fold screen.**

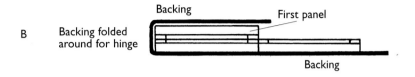

B   Backing folded
around for hinge

Backing   First panel

Backing

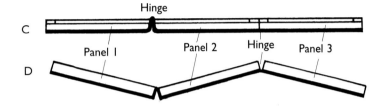

Hinge

C

Panel 1   Panel 2   Hinge   Panel 3

D

11 To assemble the panels, lay the leather, suede or vilene face down. Spread glue sparingly on the back of the second and third screen panels and place them side by side on the backing, close together. Allow the glue to dry. (*See* Fig 6.16A.)

12 Place the first screen panel on top of the second, embroidered surfaces together, and spread glue sparingly onto the backing lying beside them.

13 Wrap the backing around the edge and onto the first panel, making sure that the panel does not move. Smooth the backing into place and allow to dry (*see* Fig 6.16B). Note how the backing forms a hinge between the first and second panel and a flat join between the second and third. This allows the panels to hinge into a zig zag, whilst maintaining a very stable join (*see* Figs 6.16C and D).

14 Finally, trim away any surplus backing with a craft knife.

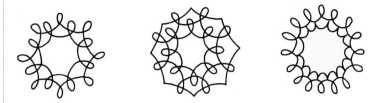

Fig 7.3 **Patterns for small mats, cloths and runners.**

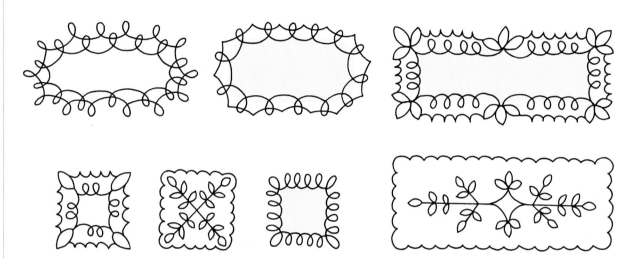

Working method

1 Trace the required patterns onto the soluble fabric and lay a piece of net fabric underneath. The shaded areas on some of the patterns indicate the position for cotton lawn or voile, a small piece of which should be cut to size and laid between the soluble fabric and the net.

2 Place both fabrics into a small ring frame.

3 Follow the instructions for embroidering with a machine as given for the lace curtains (*see* page 52).

4 Dissolve the fabrics as described for the lace curtains (*see* page 54) and trim away any surplus net from the edges.

5 Press lightly with an iron.

Working methods

1 Cut and mitre the moulding as shown in Fig 8.10A. The inner edges, **a–a** and **b–b**, are the same length as the outer edges of the completed picture or sampler.

2 Glue the sections of the frame together at each corner, taking care to wipe away any excess glue.

3 Once the glue has dried, stain and varnish as required.

Using a rebated moulding

4 Cut a piece of thin card to fit the inside of the frame rebate (*see* Fig 8.10B).

5 Cover the front of the card with a thin layer of PVA glue, wiping off any excess so that the card is just tacky.

6 Place the embroidery into position centrally on the card and gently press it onto the tacky surface (Fig 8.10C). Lay the frame over the card before the glue dries to ensure that nothing has moved, then remove.

7 Allow the glue to dry completely, then trim away the surplus fabric from around the edge.

8 Push the picture or sampler into the frame and seal the edges with narrow masking tape.

Using a plain moulding

4 Cut a piece of card 100mm (4in) square and cover it with a thin layer of PVA glue, wiping off any excess so that the card is just tacky.

5 Place the embroidery on the tacky surface and gently press it into position, in the centre of the card.

6 Allow the glue to dry completely.

Fig 8.10
Making frames and mounting pictures.

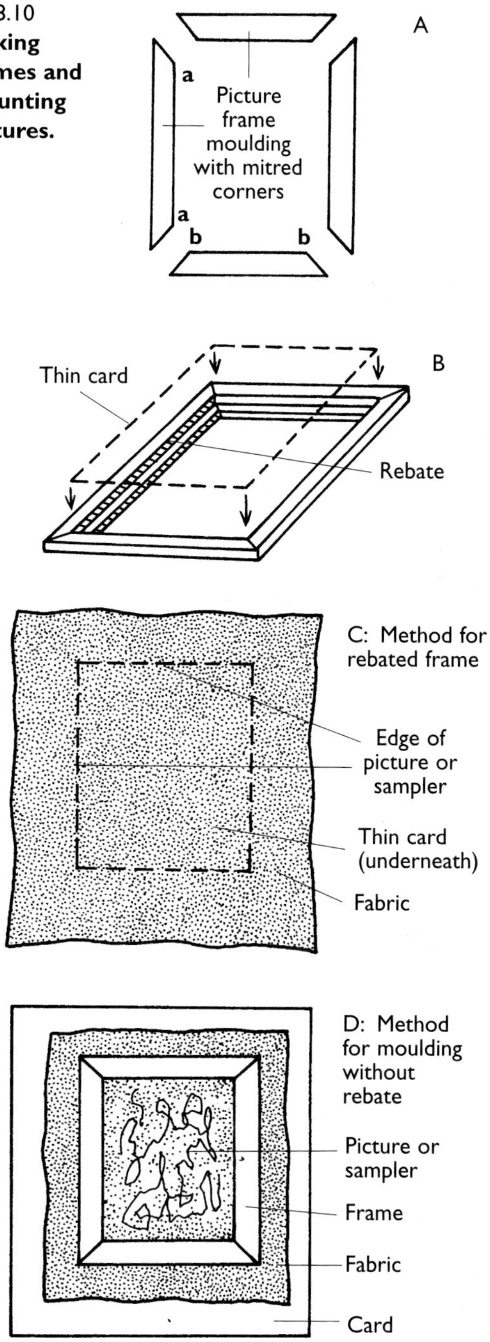

A

Picture frame moulding with mitred corners

Thin card

B

Rebate

C: Method for rebated frame

Edge of picture or sampler

Thin card (underneath)

Fabric

D: Method for moulding without rebate

Picture or sampler

Frame

Fabric

Card

7 Glue the frame into position around the picture or sampler and, once again, leave the glue to dry (Fig 8.10D).

8 With a sharp craft knife, cut away the surplus card and fabric from around the edges.

9 Bedcovers

The 'standard' bed size was not introduced until the middle of the nineteenth century. Prior to that, a bed was always made for, and to the size of, the person who would occupy it. This is why we see such a variety of beds in historic houses. However, for miniaturists' purposes, most kits and ready-made beds correspond to present-day proportions.

Most beds in the Victorian and Edwardian eras had wooden headboards and often a footboard as well, though the middle classes favoured metal bedsteads after 1851.

The sprung mattress came into use from 1855, with the tension-wired mattress following by 1890.

Four-poster beds continued to be used into the nineteenth century, with chintz or light cotton hangings popular in the 1830s. Pugin's Gothic Revival style brought ornate, heavily carved four-posters with heavy drapes. By the 1880s, however, the popularity of the four-poster waned in favour of the half-tester, until the late nineteenth century when the use of both ceased.

In early Victorian times only the more affluent households would have had sheets on all the beds.

Bedspreads hung to the floor at the sides and foot of the bed and were not necessarily padded, whereas quilts, which were padded, lay on top of the bed, possibly with a bedspread underneath them.

The following projects reflect the range of techniques that were used to make bed coverings.

Determining size

To find the correct size to make a bedcover for a particular miniature bed, follow the instructions below.

Bedspreads

Suggested sizes
Double bed
190 x 200mm (7½ x 8in)
Single bed
150 x 200mm (6 x 8in)

Working method for bedspreads

1 Place the mattress on the bed.
2 Measure the height of the bed, including the mattress, and multiply this by two.
3 Add the width of the bed to the above figure, to find the required finished width of the bedspread, excluding turnings.
4 Measure the length of the bed and add the height, including the mattress. This gives the required length for the bedspread. If there are bedposts at the foot of the bed, the corners of the quilt must be removed.

Working method for quilts

The required size for a quilt that does not hang to the floor is to the length of the bed and the width of the bed.

Quilt

Suggested sizes
Double bed
115 x 150mm (4½ x 6in)
Single bed
80 x 150mm (3 x 6in)

Fig 9.1 **Crazy patchwork quilt.**

Crazy Patchwork Bedcover

This type of patchwork, which is applied to a base fabric, was popular from the 1880s onwards.

(Instructions are given for cushions in Chapter 5, page 68.)

Working method

1 Using a fabric pen or pencil, mark the outline of the bedcover, to the required size, on the cotton square.

123

Crazy Patchwork Bedcover

Materials

Stranded cotton in bright colours, including an old gold

Fine cotton lawn, muslin or ultra light sew-in vilene interlining: 250mm (10in) square

Bond-a-web or similar: 200mm (8in) square

Silk or lightweight cotton (for lining): 250mm (10in) square

Silk or lightweight cotton scraps in bright colours

Size

As required

2 Apply the Bond-a-web within this marked outline.

3 Cut the silk or cotton into tiny, irregular pieces and lay them, mixing the colours, on the bonded area. Allow the pieces to overlap slightly and press with an iron. This will fix the pieces to the backing fabric, except for the overlapping edges. (*See* Fig 5.21.)

4 Using one strand of the old gold cotton, fix these overlapping edges with herringbone and feather stitches.

5 Using one strand of the various colours of cotton, work small flower motifs in some of the shapes with backstitch, straight stitch, detached chain stitch and French knots.

6 Trim the bedspread to the required finished size and lay it on the lining fabric.

7 Trim the lining fabric, leaving a 10mm (⅜in) border around each side, and remove a little fabric from each corner (*see* Fig 9.2A).

8 Mitre the corners, turning the edges of the lining over to form a hem on the right side of the bedspread, and secure it with small hemming stitches.

9 Press with an iron to finish.

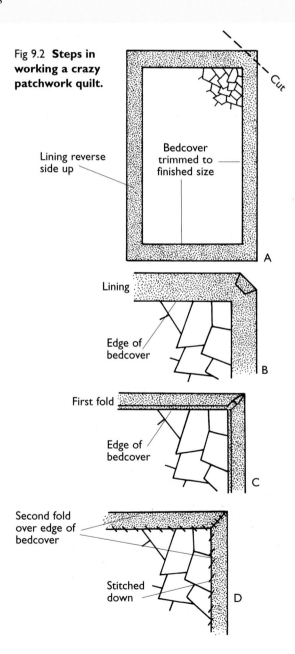

Fig 9.2 **Steps in working a crazy patchwork quilt.**

Lining reverse side up

Bedcover trimmed to finished size

Cut

A

Lining

Edge of bedcover

B

First fold

Edge of bedcover

C

Second fold over edge of bedcover

Stitched down

D

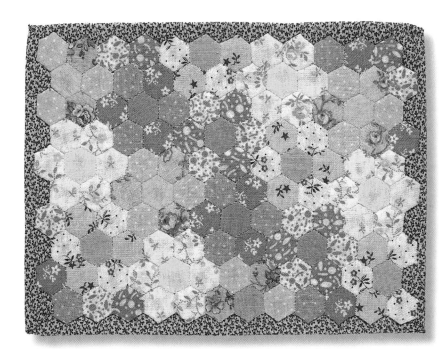

Fig 9.3 **Hexagon patchwork quilt.**

Hexagon Patchwork Bedcover

This cover uses a traditional hand-pieced patchwork method. Only fabrics of natural fibres should be used, for example, silk or light-weight cotton.

Working method

1 Determine the size of the bedcover required.

2 Trace the hexagon pattern given in Fig 5.23 (*see* page 69) and cut out a template in thin card.

3 Using this card template, cut out sufficient paper hexagons to fill a bedcover of the size

Hexagon Patchwork Bedcover

Materials

Lightweight cotton or silk in six or eight co-ordinating colours: 100mm (4in) square

Lightweight cotton or silk (for lining): 250mm (10in) square

Sewing threads, to match fabrics

Tacking cotton

Paper

Thin card

Polystyrene sheet: approx. 250mm (10in) square

Size

As required

required. To cover an area 100 x 150mm (4 x 6in) requires 120 hexagons.

4 Cut out fabric pieces to cover each paper hexagon, allowing 4mm (⅛in) turnings. Fold each side over in turn and secure with a tacking stitch (*see* Fig 5.23C–E).

5 When sufficient hexagons have been covered, they can be joined together. Place two hexagons right sides together and, with matching cotton, oversew the edges (*see* Fig 5.23E). It is helpful to pin each covered hexagon into place on the polystyrene sheet to see the pattern develop.

6 Continue joining hexagons together until groups of seven have been formed (*see* Fig 9.4). Eventually, the groups can be joined in the same way until the pattern is complete.

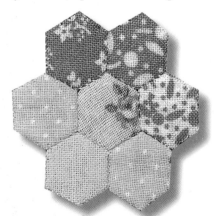

Fig 9.4 **A group of seven patches.**

7 When all the pieces have been joined, press with an iron.

8 Remove all the tacking stitches and carefully ease the papers out from each hexagon.

9 Cut the lining fabric to extend 25mm (1in) beyond the four sides of the completed hexagon bedcover, and turn the edges under 20mm (¾in) on all four sides, making a mitre at the corners (*see* Fig 9.5A).

10 Lay the lining fabric down with the turned edges uppermost (*see* Fig 9.5B), and place the completed hexagons centrally on top.

11 Stitch all around the edges with small hemming stitches, and press with an iron to finish.

Fig 9.5 **Lining and finishing a hexagon patchwork bedcover.**

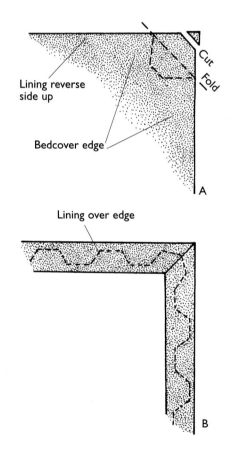

Cut
Fold

Lining reverse
side up

Bedcover edge

A

Lining over edge

B

Block Patchwork Bedcovers

Detailed instructions for constructing the Nine Patch, Little House on the Prairie and Log Cabin blocks are given in Chapter 5, where each individual block forms a cushion. For the bedcovers, each block is made up in the same way and repeated the required number of times to fill the size of bedcover desired.

Nine-Patch Bedcover

The example shown in Fig 9.6 was made using only two colours, which are reversed on alternate blocks. If desired, the blocks could be made in a variety of colours; this would require smaller pieces of fabric in a greater number of colours. Refer to the directions for the cushion on page 70 as a guide.

Working method

1 Determine the size of the bedcover required.
2 Referring to the instructions for the Nine Patch Cushion in Chapter 5 and to Fig 5.25, make up the required number of individual blocks. Cut the initial machined strips for the bedcover longer than those suggested for the cushions. Use a rotary cutter and reverse the colourways on half the blocks.

Fig 9.6 **Nine-patch bedcover.**

3 When all the blocks are complete, join them to form strips by placing adjacent blocks right sides together and stitching by hand or machine (*see* Fig 9.7A and B).

127

Nine-Patch Bedcover

Materials

Lightweight cotton or silk in main colour (for patchwork, lining and border): 500mm (19¾in) square

Lightweight cotton or silk in second colour: 300mm (12in) square

Sewing thread, to match fabrics

Quilting needle: No. 10

Suggested sizes

Each block

32mm (1¼in) square

Single bedcover: 4 x 5 blocks

Double bedcover: 6 x 6 blocks

Single quilt: 2 x 4 blocks

Double quilt: 3 x 4 blocks

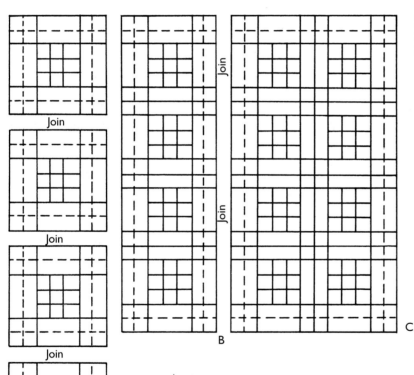

Fig 9.7 **Joining nine-patch blocks.**

4 Join these strips together in the same way (*see* Fig 9.7C) and when complete, lay the patchwork on the lining.

5 Trim the lining fabric so that there is a 10mm (⅜in) border around the patchwork and remove a little fabric from each corner, as for the crazy patchwork cover (*see* Fig 9.2A).

6 Mitre the corners and turn the edges of the lining over to form a hem on the right side of the bedspread. Secure this with small hemming stitches and press with an iron.

Fig 9.8 **Little House on the Prairie bedcover.**

Little House on the Prairie Bedcover

This was a very popular block design through-out the nineteenth century, particularly in North America.

Working method

1 Determine the size of the bedcover required.

2 Referring to the instructions for the Little House on the Prairie Cushion on page 72 and to Fig 5.27, make up the required number of blocks to fill your bedspread outline. Cut the initial machined strips longer for the bedspread than that suggested for the cushions.

3 When all the blocks are complete, cut pieces of the lining colour, 18 x 35mm (¾ x 1⅜in). Join the blocks to form strips the length of the bedcover, by inserting a piece of the lining colour between each one so that a 6mm (¼in) width shows on the right side (*see* Fig 9.9A).

Little House on the Prairie Bedcover

Materials

Lightweight cotton or silk in:

   Main colour (for lining and joining strips):
   300mm (12in) square
   Light cream and dark cream (for walls) and red (for roof):
   each 300mm (12in) square
   Light blue (for sky), dark blue (for window) and green
   (for door): each 150mm (6in) square

Sewing threads, to match fabric

Quilting needle: No. 10

Suggested sizes

Each block

18mm (¾in) square without
   the joining strip

Single bedcover: 5 x 7 blocks

Double bedcover: 6 x 7 blocks

Single quilt: 3 x 5 blocks

Double quilt: 4 x 5 blocks

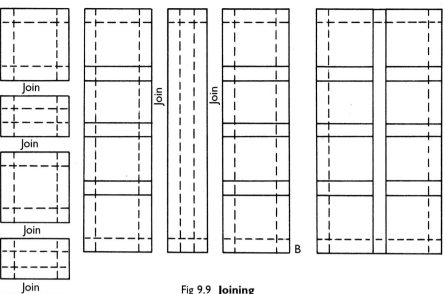

Fig 9.9 **Joining Little House on the Prairie blocks.**

4 Next, cut strips of the lining colour 18 x 200mm (¾ x 8in). Join the strips of blocks together with these lengths of lining, leaving 6mm (¼in) showing on the right side (*see* Fig 9.9B and C).

5 Finally, lay the blocks on a piece of lining. Trim the lining and turn the edges as for the Nine-Patch Bedcover (*see* page 128).

Log Cabin Bedcover

These blocks are formed with strips of fabric built up on a base and then joined. Full instructions for making the individual blocks are given in Chapter 5 for the Log Cabin Cushion (*see* page 74 and Fig 5.29).

Each block is identical in the first two options shown in Fig 9.11, with the overall patterns created by the way the blocks are placed when joined. In the third option, the order in which the colours are used differs: colours are placed on opposite sides of the square instead of adjacent sides.

Fig 9.10 **Log Cabin bedcover.**

Log Cabin Bedcover

Materials

Lightweight cotton or silk in three different colours (for patchwork design): each 300mm (12in) square *plus* additional 500mm (19¾in) square of colour chosen for lining and edges

Lightweight cotton or silk in fourth colour (for central patch of each block): 150mm (6in) square

Ultra lightweight sew-in vilene: 400mm (15¾in) square

Sewing cotton, to match fabrics

Quilting needle: No. 10

Suggested sizes

Each block

25mm (1in) square

Single bedcover: 5 x 7 blocks

Double bedcover: 6 x 7 blocks

Single quilt: 3 x 5 blocks

Double quilt: 4 x 5 blocks

Working method

1 Determine the size of the bedcover required.

2 Cut the vilene into 100mm (4in) squares. This allows four patterns to be traced on each square of vilene, with about 25mm (1in) between each pattern (*see* Fig 9.12).

3 Referring to the instructions for the Log Cabin Cushion in Chapter 5 and to Fig 5.29, make up as many blocks as are required to fill your bedspread outline.

4 When complete, join the blocks to form strips, then join the strips together, as for the Nine-Patch Bedcover (*see* page 127 and Fig 9.7).

5 Finally, line the bedcover using the same method as for the Nine-Patch Bedcover (*see* page 128) by turning a hem to the right side. Press the cover when the hem is complete.

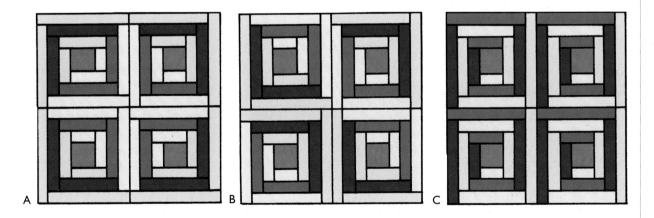

Fig 9.11 **Alternative patterns created by changing the order in which blocks are joined.**

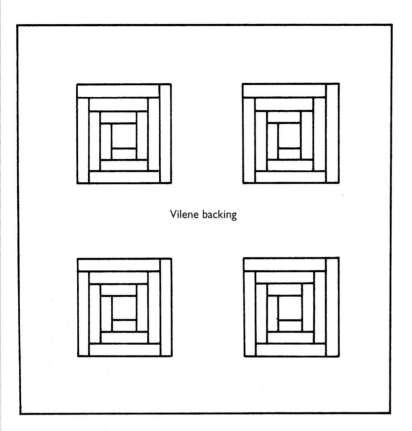

Fig 9.12 **Placement of block patterns on vilene squares.**

Vilene backing

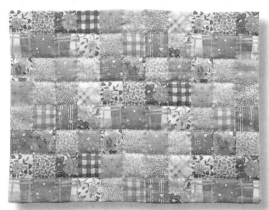

Fig 9.13
Examples of printed fabrics used to simulate patchwork.

Simulated Patchwork Bedcovers

There are a number of ways in which patchwork can be imitated which allow some of the more intricate patterns to be reproduced in miniature. Chapter 5 describes how these techniques can be used to produce cushions, while bedcovers are discussed below.

Simulated Patchwork Bedcovers

Materials

Effective ways of simulating patchwork are through the use of striped fabrics, printed fabrics, fabric transfer paints and printed geometric designs.

Size

As required

Working methods for simulating patchwork

Printed fabrics

The easiest way to simulate patchwork is by using the fabrics with a tiny patchwork print that are now available. The effect can be seen in the two examples shown in Fig 9.13.

1 Place the fabric on a layer of lightweight wadding or on four layers of muslin, with a lining of lightweight cotton or voile placed underneath the whole.
2 Secure this 'sandwich' of fabrics with tacking stitches.
3 Stitch along the outlines of the printed design with small running stitches, using a matching sewing thread.
4 When complete, trim the wadding or muslin back to just within the edges of the bedcover (*see* Fig 9.21A).
5 Turn under the top fabric and the lining so that both lie inside the edge of the bedcover (*see* Fig 9.21B), and stitch the edges of the two fabrics together to form a hem on the right side. Press to finish.

Fig 9.14 **Striped fabric used to simulate patchwork.**

Striped fabrics

An impression of patchwork made of square pieces can be given by using striped fabric. The stripes in the fabric must be of equal width.

1 Cut the fabric into strips across the stripes.
2 Join the strips together, having moved each stripe to meet another colour.
3 Finish the bedcover following the method given for the Nine-Patch Bedcover (*see* page 128).

133

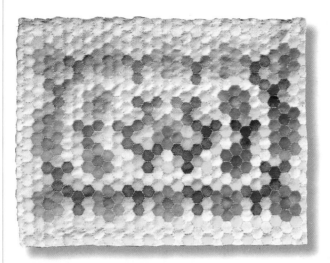

Fig 9.15 **Fabric transfer paints used to simulate patchwork.**

Fabric transfer paints

A third method, which is ideal for miniature work, is the use of fabric transfer paints (*see* Chapter 13, page 171). These paints are designed to be used on synthetic fabrics and give the best colours when used on these. The colours change when ironed off onto fabric, so prepare a sample strip as described in Chapter 13.

The advantage of using this method is that a true representation of patchwork, in the correct miniature scale, can be reproduced.

Two patterns are given in Figs 9.16a and b, but any pattern desired can be drawn onto paper. Photocopy paper is ideal. The patterns given can be photocopied and, if necessary, joined to make the size required.

1 Paint the pattern shapes with fabric transfer paints in a variety of colours (*see* Fig 9.15).

Fig 9.16a **Block pattern for 'painted patchwork'.**

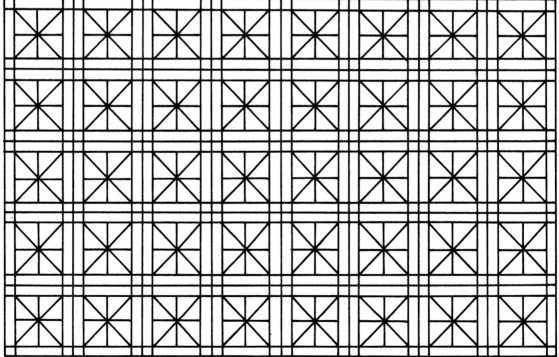

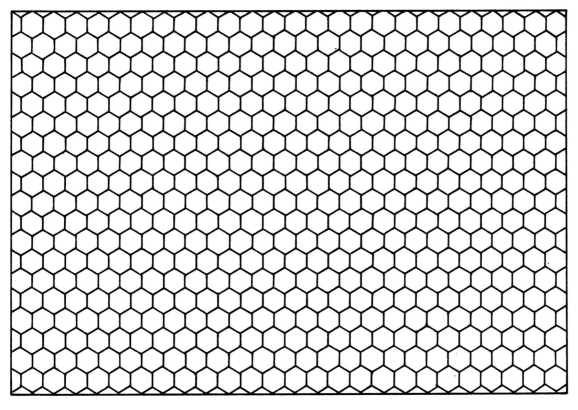

Fig 9.16b **Hexagon pattern for 'painted patchwork'.**

2 Leave to dry completely, then iron off the transfer onto your fabric.

3 Prepare the fabric with layers of wadding or muslin and a lining, as described for the printed fabric bedcover (*see* page 133), and secure it with tacking stitches.

4 Outline the shapes in the pattern with tiny running stitches.

5 When complete, line and finish the bedcover, again following the method given for the printed fabric bedcover (*see* page 133).

Fig 9.17 **Mock appliqué bedcover.**

Mock Appliqué Bedcover

True appliqué is too bulky to use for miniatures, but a printed, bonded fabric can be used to great effect.

Working method

1 Press all fabrics to remove creases.

2 Mark the finished size of the bedcover on the main fabric, with tacking stitches.

3 Select pieces of the printed fabric that have flowers and leaves that are suitable for cutting out as motifs. Bond a piece of Bond-a-web to the reverse sides of these pieces then cut out the flower and leaf motifs and peel off the paper backing.

4 Lay the motifs on the main fabric to create the desired design. This can be formal and symmetrical, perhaps a central group and a

Mock Appliqué Bedcover

Materials	Size
Lightweight cotton, silk or polyester: 250mm (10in) square	As required
Transparent nylon, chiffon or organza: 250mm (10in) square	
Fabric scraps, with very small printed flowers	
Bond-a-web or similar	
Sewing cotton, to match main fabric	
Quilting needle: No. 10	

border (*see* Fig 9.17), or the motifs can be scattered in a random way. When you are happy with the effect, place a sheet of non-stick baking paper over the fabric and press all the pieces with an iron to bond them into place.

5 Lay the transparent fabric over the whole bedcover and stitch around all the motifs, through all the layers, with a tiny running stitch.

6 Finally, turn a narrow hem, folding the main and transparent fabrics as one, and secure with tiny hemming stitches.

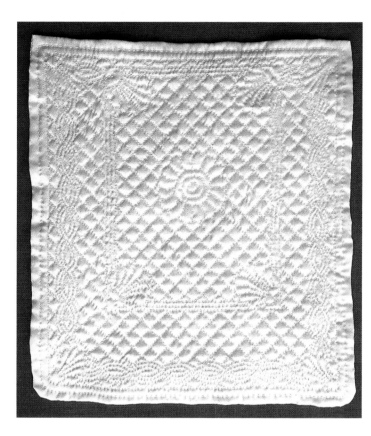

Fig 9.18 **Quilted double bedspread.**

Fig 9.19 **Quilted double quilt.**

Quilted Bedcovers

Quilting was popular for bedcovers and quilts throughout the Victorian era. For miniature scale, only the softest fabrics are successful, for example, silk, crepe-backed satins of silk or polyester, cotton voile or fine cotton lawn. Figures 9.18–9.20 shows quilted designs to suit covers of different sizes.

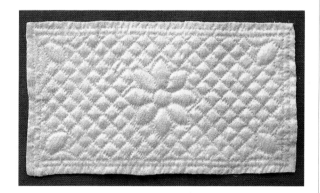

Fig 9.20 **Quilted single quilt.**

137

Quilted Bedcovers

Materials

Fabric (as suggested above): 250mm (10in) square

Lightweight cotton lawn or voile (for lining): 250mm (10in) square

Muslin: 250mm (10in) square x 4 OR

Lightweight wadding: 250mm (10in) square

Sewing thread, to match top fabric

Quilting needle: No. 10

Size

As for selected pattern

Working method

1 Press all fabrics to remove creases.

2 Select and photocopy the required design, then transfer the design by ironing the photocopy onto the lining. Alternatively, lay the lining over the design and trace it with a fabric pencil. (For details of these methods *see* Chapter 12, pages 167 and 168.)

3 Lay the muslin or wadding between the top fabric and the lining, making sure that the design on the lining can be seen. Secure these layers with tacking stitches worked diagonally.

4 Beginning in the centre of the design, follow all the lines with a tiny running stitch, stitching from the back of the bedcover. Begin and fasten off the threads by taking the needle between the layers, and cutting off the thread wherever it emerges. Do not work the lines around the outside edges as these form part of the making up process.

5 When the quilting is complete, trim the muslin or wadding back to just within the outside edges of the bedcover (*see* Fig 9.21A), and turn under both the top fabric and the lining so that both allowances are inside the edge of the bedcover (*see* Fig 9.21B). Stitch together the edges of the two fabrics.

6 Finally, complete any quilting around the edge to hold the hem flat (Fig 9.21C).

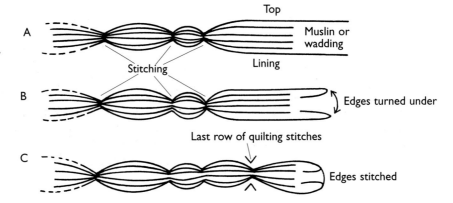

Fig 9.21 **Finishing the edges of quilted bedcovers.**

Top

A

Muslin or wadding

Stitching

Lining

B

Edges turned under

Last row of quilting stitches

C

Edges stitched

Fig 9.22 **Pattern for white bed cover shown in Fig 9.18.**

Fig 9.23 **Pattern for blue and peach quilts shown in Figs 9.19 and 9.20.**

Fig 9.24
**Embroidered
bedspread.**

Embroidered
Bedspread

The design for this project is based on a bedcover at Kelmscott Manor which was designed by William Morris and worked by Morris and his wife Jane. The original cover was worked on a homespun linen with silk embroidery. The bed at Kelmscott, for which it was made, is a heavy, Gothic revival four-poster with embroidered bed curtains.

Embroidered Bedspread

Materials

Stranded cotton as listed in colour key

Lightweight cotton or voile, pale cream: 250mm (10in) square

Embroidery or crewel needle: No. 10

Round or rectangular frame

Size

193 x 200mm ($7\frac{5}{8}$ x 8in)

NB: This pattern can be adjusted to fit any bed: measuring from the centre to the nearest complete floral motif each side, add or subtract the number of motifs necessary

141

Fig 9.25 **Pattern for embroidered bedspread.**

142

The pattern given for this miniature bedcover could be adapted for use on bed curtains if desired, or the cover could be accompanied by plain curtains as shown in the William Morris room setting (*see* page 57).

Preparation

Transfer the design to the fabric. Either photocopy the pattern and iron the copy onto the fabric (this reverses the design, but it is very easy and quick to do), or lay the fabric over the

Embroidered Bedspread		Skeins	DMC	Anchor	Madeira
Leaves and berries					
	Light grey green	1	504	1042	1701
	Dark grey green	1	502	876	1703
	Dark red	1	815	43	0512
'Tulip'					
	Bright pink	1	892	28	0412
	Bronze green	1	832	907	2202
'Rose'					
	Dark red	1	815	43	0512
	Pink	1	223	895	0812
	Dark grey green	1	502	876	1703
Yellow 'daisy'					
	Yellow	1	725	305	0106
	Bronze green	1	832	907	2202
	Olive green	1	937	268	1504
Pink 'daisy'					
	Salmon pink	1	352	9	0303
	Olive green	1	937	268	1504
Blue flower					
	Blue	1	813	161	1013
	Green	1	472	264	1414
Trellis					
	Tan	1	3046	887	2206

Fig 9.26 **Stitch pattern for embroidered bedspread.**

pattern and trace the design with a fabric pencil or soluble pen. Details of both methods are given in Chapter 12 (*see* page 168).

Mount the fabric into a round or rectangular frame as desired.

Working method

Refer to Figs 9.24 and 9.26 for the placement of stitches and colours. Use one strand of stranded cotton throughout and begin with a small knot and double stitch.

Work the petals of the yellow flowers in detached chain stitch, with French knots for their centres. Work the pink flowers in detached chain stitch as well and the rose with three small

pink straight stitches inside each petal and centre. The berries, again, are French knots. The rest of the design is worked in backstitch.

Do not work the two lines that form the border as they are used to make the hem.

When the embroidery is complete, trim the fabric to 25mm (1in) all round the edge. Turn the four edges under to the reverse side, just outside the outer line of the design, and mitre each corner. (This is similar to the lining for the Hexagon Bedcover, *see* Fig 9.5.)

Now work the backstitch border, taking the stitches through the hem. Trim the surplus fabric back close to the stitching and press with an iron.

10 Small decorative items

The Victorians were fond of filling their rooms with decorative things of all kinds: ornaments, pictures, lamps, plants and especially embroidered items. If it was possible to add fringes, tassels and beads, so much the better.

There would be covers on all available surfaces and a valance along the mantelpiece – even in the kitchen. The gentlemen of the house would be presented with embroidered slippers, braces, waistcoats and watch pockets by their dutiful daughters.

This chapter covers a few of the items which would have been found throughout the Victorian and Edwardian eras.

Edwardian room setting.

Fig 10.1 **Garland mantel valance.**

Fig 10.2 **Van Dyke mantel valance.**

Mantel Valances

It was fashionable throughout the Victorian period, and through to the 1930s, to hang a valance along the edge of the mantelpiece.

The Garland design in Fig 10.1 suits the early and late Victorian house, while the Van Dyke design in Fig 10.2 suits the 1860s and 1870s. During Edwardian times, mantel valances were embroidered with floral sprays or decorated with a braid.

Preparation

Measure the width of the fireplace mantel to find the length of valance required. The width of the valance should be between 10 and 25mm (⅜ and 1in), depending on the style of the fireplace.

Mantel Valances

Materials	Sizes
For each valance	As required

Stranded cotton as listed in colour key

Ribbon, 10mm (⅜in) wide: 200mm (8in)

Tapestry needle: No. 26 or 28

For Garland design

Evenweave linen (35 count), painted with fabric dye: 200 x 50mm (8 x 2in)

For Van Dyke design

Evenweave cotton (28 count), painted with fabric dye: 200 x 50mm (8 x 2in)

NB: Both designs could be worked on any count from 27 to 40, with the
final size of the piece varying accordingly

Mark the outline and the centre of the valance on the fabric with lines of tacking thread (*see* Fig 10.3).

Working method

Following the relevant chart, begin working from the centre in tent stitch with one strand of stranded cotton. Work as many repeats of the pattern as are required to fill the length. This will depend on what count of fabric is being used and on how wide the mantelpiece is.

Making up

Trim the fabric on all sides to about 6mm (¼in). Fold the top and bottom edges (the longer edges) to the reverse of the design and press with an iron. Next, trim a small amount of the excess turning from each corner.

Now fold the two sides (the short ends) to the reverse of the fabric. Tuck the ends of the turnings under, lay the ribbon over the turnings, and secure it with small hemming stitches (*see* Fig 10.6).

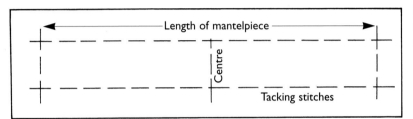

Fig 10.3 **Measuring and marking the valance outline.**

Mantel Valances

		Skeins	DMC	Anchor	Madeira
	Gold	I	725	305	0106
	Dark peach	I	352	9	0303
	Red	I	666	9046	0210
	Dark red	I	815	43	0512
	Light rose pink	I	818	271	0608
	Mid rose pink	I	776	24	0607
	Dark rose pink	I	892	28	0412
	Mauve	I	553	99	0711
	Green	I	470	266	1410

Fig 10.4 **Chart for Garland design.**

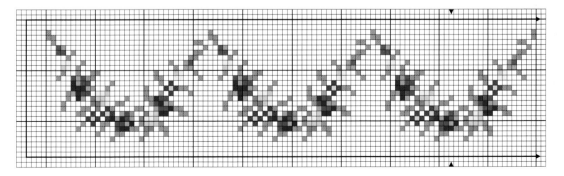

147

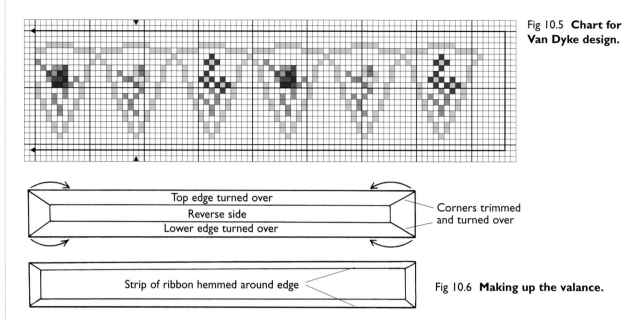

Fig 10.5 **Chart for Van Dyke design.**

Fig 10.6 **Making up the valance.**

Top edge turned over

Reverse side

Lower edge turned over

Corners trimmed and turned over

Strip of ribbon hemmed around edge

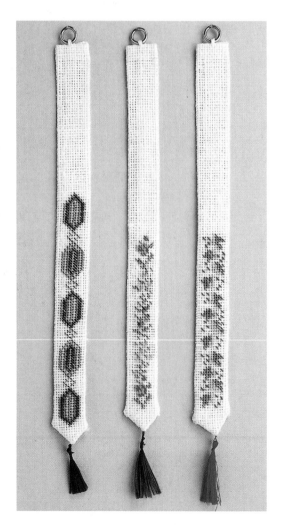

Press the valance with an iron, and attach the valance to the mantelpiece with a small amount of glue or Grip-wax.

Bell Pulls

A bell pull can be hung near a fireplace or a door. The Floral Spray and Berries designs are suited to the whole Victorian era, but the Geometric design is more suited to the 1880s.

Preparation

Mount the fabric in a card frame (*see* Chapter 12, page 166). Mark the sides of the bell pull on the fabric with two lines of tacking stitch: there will be 13 threads between them.

Fig 10.7 **Bell pulls. From left: Geometric, Floral Spray and Berries designs.**

Bell Pulls

Materials

Stranded cotton as listed in colour key

Evenweave linen (35 count): 150 x 50mm (6 x 2in)

Tapestry needle: No. 26 or 28

Tiny curtain ring

Fabric glue

Card frame

Size

10 x 100mm

($^3/_8$ x 4in)

Floral Spray Bell Pull

		Skeins	DMC	Anchor	Madeira
	Green	I	502	876	1703
	Pink	I	352	9	0303
	Red	I	666	9046	0210
	Yellow	I	444	297	0105
	Orange	I	740	316	0202
	Light mauve	I	554	96	0711
	Mid mauve	I	553	99	0712
	Dark mauve	I	550	102	0713
	Blue	I	799	145	0910

Berries Bell Pull

		Skeins	DMC	Anchor	Madeira
	Dark green	I	470	266	1410
	Light green	I	472	264	1414
	Red	I	666	9046	0210

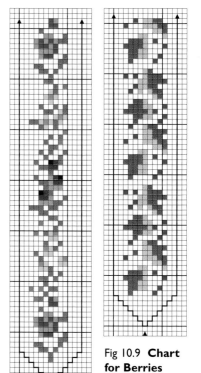

Fig 10.9 **Chart for Berries design.**

Fig 10.8 **Chart for Floral Spray design.**

Working method

Following the desired chart, begin the design at the lower end of the bell pull, and use tent stitch with one strand of cotton throughout. Leave at least 25mm (1in) of fabric below the embroidery for turnings.

Repeat the pattern however many times you require. The length of the bell pull can be adjusted according to the height of the room.

149

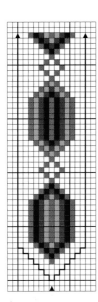

Geometric Bell Pull		Skeins	DMC	Anchor	Madeira
	Green	1	502	876	1703
	Light mauve	1	554	96	0711
	Mid mauve	1	553	99	0712
	Dark mauve	1	550	102	0713

Fig 10.10 **Chart for Geometric design.**

Fig 10.11 **Making up the bell pulls.**

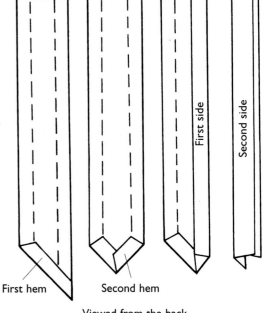

Viewed from the back

Making up

Trim the side edges to 6mm (¼in). Shape the upper and lower ends as shown in Fig 10.11 and secure the turnings using fabric glue, very sparingly. Next, turn one side edge under and glue it down, then repeat for the second edge.

Make a small tassel (*see* Chapter 4, page 46 and Fig 4.14) and attach it to the lower pointed edge of the bell pull.

Finally, stitch a small curtain ring in the centre of the top edge, for hanging.

Needlework Boxes

Embroidery was considered a responsible way for a young lady to occupy her time. Many workboxes would have been in the form of a small piece of furniture, but a smaller work basket was more portable.

Fig 10.12 **Needlework boxes. Clockwise from right: Designs A, B, C and D.**

The designs presented here are for needlework boxes in two sizes.

Cutting list for large box
Lid: 32 x 22mm (1¼ x ⅞in)

x–x 6mm (¼in)

Base: 32 x 22mm (1¼ x ⅞in)

x–x 10mm (⅜in)

Divider: 50 x 21mm (2 x ¹³⁄₁₆in)

Cutting list for small box
Lid: 28 x 20mm (1⅛ x ¾in)

x–x 6mm (¼in)

Base: 28 x 20mm (1⅛ x ¾in)

x–x 10mm (⅜in)

Divider: 50 x 19mm (2 x ¾in)

Preparation
Select the size of box desired, and mark the canvas with tacking lines as indicated in Fig 10.17A.

Working method
Following the relevant chart, work the design on one half of the canvas, in cross stitch, using one strand of stranded cotton.

When the stitching is complete, cut the fabric into separate pieces along the line z–z. The small, lower piece will be used to make a hinge. Trim the corners of the fabric as shown in Fig 10.17B.

Making up
Mark and cut out the card for the base and lid as indicated in the cutting list. Score the dotted lines and cut away the corners (*see* Fig 10.17D).

Needlework Boxes

Materials	Sizes
For each box	**Large**
Stranded cotton as listed in colour key	32 x 22 x 16mm
Mono canvas (22 or 24 count): 100mm (4in) square	(1¼ x ⅞ x ⅝in)
Lightweight printed cotton (for lining): 100mm (4in) square	**Small**
Tapestry needle: No. 26 or 28	28 x 20 x 16mm
Bond-a-web or similar: 100mm (4in) square	(1⅛ x ¾ x ⅝in)
Narrow braid or ribbon: 300mm (12in)	
Bead	
Brass pin	
PVA glue	
Thin card: 200mm (8in) square	
Paper strip: 6 x 300mm (¼ x 12in)	

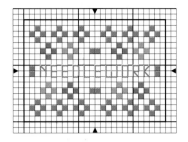

Fig 10.13 Chart for Needlework box, Design A.

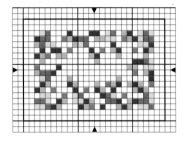

Fig 10.14 Chart for Needlework box, Design B.

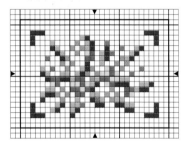

Fig 10.15 Chart for Needlework box, Design C.

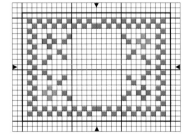

Fig 10.16 Chart for Needlework box, Design D.

Needlework Boxes – Design 1

		Skeins	DMC	Anchor	Madeira
	Bright green	1	702	226	1306
	Dark pink	1	892	28	0412
	Mauve	1	554	96	0711

Needlework Boxes – Design 2

		Skeins	DMC	Anchor	Madeira
	Light green	1	3013	854	1605
	Dark green	1	3011	924	1607
	Light pink	1	353	868	0304
	Dark pink	1	892	28	0412
	Blue	1	799	145	0910

Needlework Boxes – Design 3

		Skeins	DMC	Anchor	Madeira
	Bright green	1	702	226	1306
	Dark pink	1	892	28	0412
	Mauve	1	554	96	0711
	Pale yellow	1	3078	292	0102

Needlework Boxes – Design 4

		Skeins	DMC	Anchor	Madeira
	Light green	1	3013	854	1605
	Dark green	1	3011	924	1607
	Light pink	1	353	868	0304
	Dark pink	1	892	28	0412
	Mauve	1	554	96	0711
	Pale yellow	1	3078	292	0102
	Blue	1	799	145	0910

Note that the scored lines are on the *outside* of the box. Mark and cut out the card for the divider. Score a line in the centre, and one 6mm (¼in) either side of the centre (*see* Fig 10.17E). Iron the Bond-a-web to the reverse side of the printed cotton. Bond a piece of fabric to the *inside* of the lid and base and to one side of the divider. Place a piece of non-stick baking paper

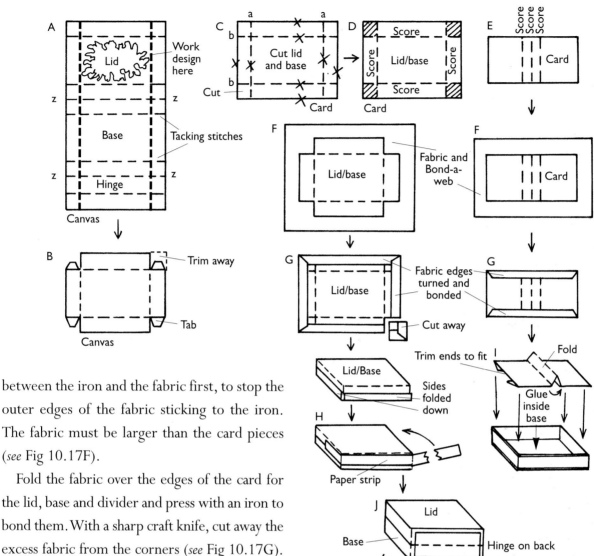

between the iron and the fabric first, to stop the outer edges of the fabric sticking to the iron. The fabric must be larger than the card pieces (*see* Fig 10.17F).

Fold the fabric over the edges of the card for the lid, base and divider and press with an iron to bond them. With a sharp craft knife, cut away the excess fabric from the corners (*see* Fig 10.17G). Next, fold down the sides of the lid and base along the scored lines, and secure by gluing a strip of paper round the edges. Make sure that the corners are square (*see* Fig 10.17H).

Fold the divider along the scored lines and glue to hold (*see* Fig 10.17I). Leave to dry completely. When it has dried, place it over the base and trim the divider so that it fits inside the base. Insert and secure with a little glue.

Place the lid and base together. Cut the hinge to size and glue it onto the back (*see* Fig 10.17J). Leave to dry.

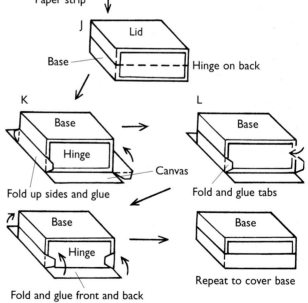

Fig 10.17 **Making up the needlework boxes.**

153

Next, place the decorated canvas over the lid and bend the sides into position, trimming the edges to fit as necessary. Glue the canvas into place, taking the tabs around the corner as shown in Figs 10.17K and 10.17L. Once this has dried, fold the ends into place, trimming as before, and glue.

Cover the base with the plain piece of canvas in the same way. Cut the brass pin down to 6mm (¼in), thread a bead onto the pin, and then glue it into the front of the base, just below the centre.

Take a strand from the canvas and make a small loop with it. Glue this loop on the front of the lid, so that it sits above the bead and can be used as a latch.

To finish, glue a narrow braid or ribbon around the top of the base and the bottom of the lid (*see* Fig 10.12).

Fig 10.18 **Watch pockets.**
From left: Designs A, C and B.

Watch Pockets

These little 'pockets' were made to hang on the wall next to the chair occupied by a gentleman.

He could then place his pocket watch into it whilst relaxing.

Watch Pockets

Materials
For each design
Stranded cotton as listed in the colour key
Evenweave linen (35 count): 100mm (4in) square
Thin suede, leather or felt
Tapestry needle: No. 26 or 28
Thin card
PVA glue

Sizes
As for pattern

The examples shown were worked on evenweave linen coloured with fabric dyes. (This process is covered in Chapter 13: *see* page 171). The amount of fabric listed is more than enough to make one watch pocket, but it is difficult to work on smaller pieces.

Fig 10.19 **Pattern for watch pockets.**

Preparation

Trace off the pattern from Fig 10.19 and use it as a template to mark out the main shape and the pocket on the fabric, with tacking stitches.

Working method

Following the required chart, work the embroidery in tent stitch, using one strand of stranded cotton.

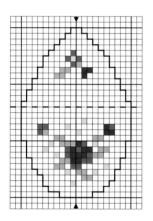

Fig 10.20 **Chart for watch pocket, Design A.**

Fig 10.21 **Chart for watch pocket, Design B.**

Watch Pockets – Design 1

		Skeins	DMC	Anchor	Madeira
	Green	1	702	226	1306
	Red	1	321	47	0510
	Dark red	1	915	1029	0705
	Yellow	1	444	297	0105

Alternative backgrounds (if fabric not dyed)

		Skeins	DMC	Anchor	Madeira
	Blue	1	798	137	0911
	Red	1	815	43	0512
	Green	1	937	268	1504
	Black	1	310	403	Black

Watch Pockets – Design 2

		Skeins	DMC	Anchor	Madeira
	Light grey	1	762	234	1804
	Mid grey	1	318	399	1802
	Dark grey	1	413	236	1713

Alternative backgrounds (if fabric not dyed)

		Skeins	DMC	Anchor	Madeira
	Blue	1	798	137	0911
	Red	1	815	43	0512
	Green	1	937	268	1504
	Black	1	310	403	Black

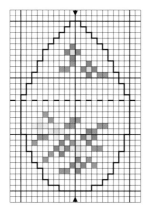

Fig 10.22 **Chart for watch pocket, Design C.**

Watch Pockets – Design 3

		Skeins	DMC	Anchor	Madeira
	Green	1	702	226	1306
	Light pink	1	3326	36	0606
	Red	1	321	47	0510
	Yellow	1	444	297	0105

Alternative backgrounds (if fabric not dyed)

		Skeins	DMC	Anchor	Madeira
	Blue	1	798	137	0911
	Red	1	815	43	0512
	Green	1	937	268	1504
	Black	1	310	403	Black

Making up

Use the template you made above to mark out the pattern onto a piece of thin card.

Cut out the two embroidered shapes, allowing a 5mm (³⁄₁₆in) turning. Place the larger embroidered section over the card shape, cut small snips around the edge of the fabric, and fold the edges over to the back of the card. Secure with fabric glue (*see* Fig 10.23). Allow this to dry completely before trimming away any surplus fabric.

Next, fold the straight upper edge of the pocket section under and secure with a little fabric glue. Place this section into position over the covered card, fold the edges to the back of the card, and glue to hold. Again, allow this to dry completely before trimming away the surplus fabric.

Add a small loop of fabric to the top corner and, finally, cover the back with a small piece of thin suede, leather or felt.

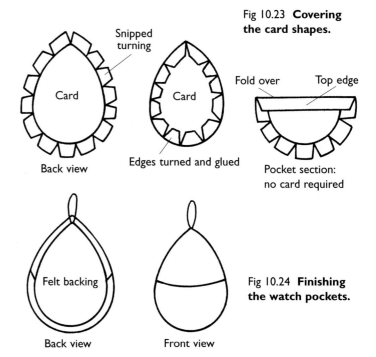

Fig 10.23 **Covering the card shapes.**

Fig 10.24 **Finishing the watch pockets.**

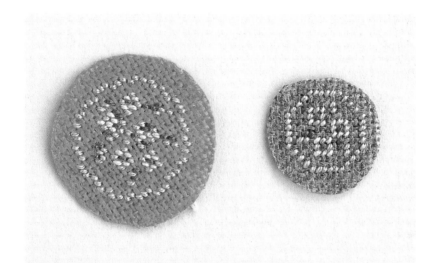

Fig 10.25 **Pot stands.**

Pot Stands

The two little pot stands shown here are worked using the centre parts of the charts for the grisaille footstools (*see* Figs 5.45 and 5.46). Any of the small floral motifs in the Van Dyke Mantel Valance on page 148, or from the cushions in Chapter 5, could be picked out and used in the same way.

Preparation

Paint the fabric with fabric paints and allow to dry. Place a small coin on the fabric and trace around it with a fabric pencil.

Working method

Work the chosen motif in the centre in tent stitch, using one strand of cotton. When the stitching is complete, carefully cut the pot stand out just within the traced pencil line.

To finish, seal the edges with a little fabric glue or Fray-check.

Pot Stands

Materials	Sizes
Stranded cotton as listed in colour key for Grisaille Footstool	As required
Evenweave linen (35 count): 100mm (4in) square	
Tapestry needle: No. 26 or 28	
Fabric glue or Fray-check	

Fig 10.26 **Hanging letter cases.**

Fig 10.27 **Pattern for hanging letter case.**

Upper back	
	Fold
	Fold
	Fold
	Fold
	Fold
	Fold
	Fold
	Fold
	Fold
Lower back	

Hanging Letter Cases

These pretty little letter cases were made by ladies to hang on the wall to hold letters awaiting a reply.

Preparation

Lay the ribbon on the pattern in Fig 10.27 and lightly mark the edge of the ribbon on the dotted fold lines. Iron the Bond-a-web onto the back of the ribbon, and remove the paper backing.

Hanging Letter Cases

Materials

Stranded cotton, in colours to contrast with ribbon

Soft ribbon, 22mm (⅞in) wide: 180mm (7in)

Embroidery or crewel needle: No. 10

Bond-a-web or similar: 180mm (7in) square

Small curtain ring (optional)

Sizes

As for pattern

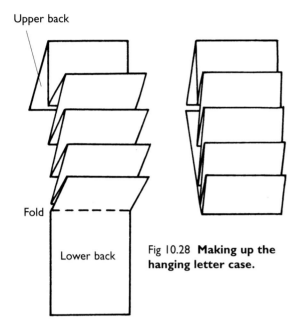

Upper back

Fold

Lower back

Fig 10.28 **Making up the hanging letter case.**

Working method

Work the embroidery in the positions indicated in Fig 10.27, referring to the photograph in Fig 10.26 as a guide. Using one strand of cotton, work detached chain stitch for the leaves and petals and French knots for the centres.

Making up

When the embroidery is complete, fold the ribbon as indicated in Fig 10.28. Press with an iron to bond the folds into place.

Finally, add a small curtain ring or loop of thread to the top edge, for hanging.

Nightdress Cases

The nightdress case provided another opportunity for a young Victorian or Edwardian lady to demonstrate her ability to embroider. The case would be displayed on the bed, providing discreet storage, out of sight, for a nightgown.

Preparation

Lay the ribbon on the pattern in Fig 10.30. Lightly mark the edges of the ribbon on the dotted fold lines, and trace the design onto the fabric with a fabric pencil.

Iron the Bond-a-web to the reverse side of the ribbon and peel off the paper backing.

Working method

Work the embroidery, using one strand of stranded cotton, in back stitch, detached chain stitch and French knots. Refer to the photograph in Fig 10.29 as a guide.

Fig 10.29 **Nightdress cases.**

159

Nightdress Cases

Materials

Stranded cotton, in colours to contrast with ribbon

Soft ribbon, approx. 38mm (1½in) wide: 200mm (8in)

Embroidery or crewel needle: No. 10

Bond-a-web or similar: 200mm (8in) square

Sizes

As for pattern

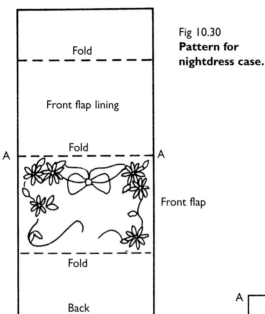

Fig 10.30
Pattern for nightdress case.

Making up

When the embroidery is complete, fold on the lines **a**–**a**, and press with an iron to seal the Bond-a-web (*see* Fig 10.31). Next, fold on the line **b**–**b**, and press again.

Sew up the side seam with tiny oversewing stitches and finally, fold on the line **c**–**c** to form a flap. Press to bond.

A small bead and loop for fastening can be stitched into place if required.

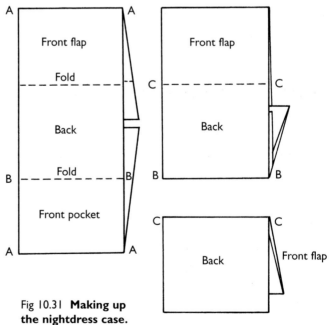

Fig 10.31 **Making up the nightdress case.**

11 Working to 1/24 scale

Many of the projects in this book are suitable for working in 1/24 scale. The following chart lists the fabric and threads needed to work the projects in this scale, and the resultant size of the finished pieces. The methods remain the same as for 1/12 scale.

The curtains, embroidered screens, embroidered bedcover and plain linen only need the patterns reduced. The fabrics and threads remain much the same as for 1/12 scale. However, it is crucial that only very lightweight fabrics are used; preferably cotton or silk.

The method for reproducing patchwork with fabric transfer paints works well in this smaller scale, and patterns can be reduced on a photocopier.

Some of the embroidered cushions and small embroidered items worked on plain fabric are very difficult to reduce as it is hard to work the stitching to scale, but if you want to try … why not!

Counted thread work

Suitable fabrics for projects based on counted threads include 40 count evenweave linen and 40 or 80 count silk gauze. Mount a piece of the required size in a card window mount as shown in Chapter 12 (*see* page 166).

Projects should be worked in one strand of stranded cotton, unless otherwise stated. The stitches used for the 1/12 scale pieces remain the same. Use a No. 28 tapestry needle for all the designs.

Item	Fabric count	Thread	Approximate size mm	in
Early Victorian Carpet	40	Stranded cotton	112 x 74	$4\frac{3}{8}$ x $2\frac{7}{8}$
	80	Stranded cotton	56 x 38	$2\frac{3}{16}$ x $1\frac{1}{2}$
Late Victorian Carpet	40	Stranded cotton	122 x 61	$4\frac{13}{16}$ x $2\frac{3}{8}$
	80	Stranded cotton	61 x 43	$2\frac{3}{8}$ x $1\frac{11}{16}$
Arts and Crafts Carpet	40	Stranded cotton	102 x 51	$4\frac{1}{32}$ x 2
	80	Stranded cotton	51 x 25	2 x 1
Stair Carpet One	40	Stranded cotton	23 wide	$\frac{7}{8}$ wide
Stair Carpet Two	40	Stranded cotton	23 wide	$\frac{7}{8}$ wide
Stair Carpet Three	40	Stranded cotton	20 wide	$\frac{3}{4}$ wide
Couched Rugs	N/A	Perlé 5 Perlé 8 Fine wool	As desired	
Plaited Rugs	N/A	Perlé 8 Perlé 12 Fine wool	As desired	
Darned Rugs	40	Stranded cotton	As desired	
Canvas Rug One	40	Stranded cotton	38 x 19	$1\frac{1}{2}$ x $\frac{3}{4}$
Canvas Rug Two	40	Stranded cotton	33 x 18	$1\frac{3}{8}$ x $\frac{11}{16}$
Canvas Rug Three	40	Stranded cotton	43 x 23	$1\frac{11}{16}$ x $\frac{7}{8}$
Canvaswork Cushions: Vase, Rose Spray and Cat	40 80	Stranded cotton Stranded cotton	23 square 12.5 square	$\frac{7}{8}$ square $\frac{1}{2}$ square
Canvaswork Cushions: Floral Posy, Garland and Grisaille	40 80	Stranded cotton Stranded cotton	18 square 9 square	$\frac{11}{16}$ square $\frac{5}{16}$ square

Item	Fabric count	Thread	Approximate size	
			mm	in
Embroidered and Painted Patchwork Cushions	N/A	Stranded cotton	13 or 19 square	½ or ¾ square
Florentine Chair Seats	80	Stranded cotton	Work to outline	
Canvaswork Chair Seats	40	Stranded cotton	Work to outline	
	80	Stranded cotton	Work to outline	
Pole Screens:				
Oval Posy	80	Stranded cotton	15 x 10	⅝ x ⅜
Peacock	80	Stranded cotton	16 square	⅝ square
Geometric	80	Stranded cotton	16 x 14	⅝ x ⁹⁄₁₆
Fire Screens:				
Peacock	36	Stranded cotton	25 x 26	1 x 1$\frac{1}{32}$
Geometric	36	Stranded cotton	26 x 30	1$\frac{1}{32}$ x 1$\frac{3}{16}$
Folding Screen:				
Oval Posy	40	Stranded cotton	29 x 19	1⅛ x ¾
Tablecloths and covers	N/A	N/A	Overhang allowance 20	Overhang allowance ¾
Pictures	40	Stranded cotton	33 x 25	1$\frac{5}{16}$ x 1
	80	Stranded cotton	16 x 12	⅝ x $\frac{7}{16}$
Samplers	80	Stranded cotton	Various	Various
Small items	80	Stranded cotton	Various	Various

12 Frames and transfer of designs

Embroidery Frames

Most of the projects in this book will benefit from being worked in an embroidery frame. When working on canvas and evenweave fabrics, the frame will help to reduce distortion. It is also easier to be precise with the stitching when the fabric is stabilized in a frame.

There are various types of frame: slate frames, stretchers, card mounts and tambour (round) frames. Each requires a different method of preparation, as described below.

When using canvas or coin net, always use a rectangular slate frame or stretcher as the canvas will distort badly in a round frame. Evenweave, silk and cotton fabrics can be used in rectangular or round frames.

For very small items, such as pictures, samplers and watch pockets, mount the fabric in a small card frame: this will accommodate a small piece of fabric without waste.

Slate frames

These are rectangular frames consisting of two flat sides and two rounded sides. The rounded sides have a strip of webbing, onto which the fabric is sewn. The flat sides have circular notches at either end, into which the rounded sides are slotted. The tension of the fabric is adjusted by rolling the rounded sides and, once correct, is held by wing nuts located at each corner.

Fig 12.1 **Using a slate frame.**

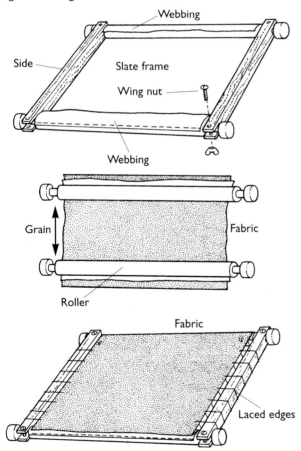

Fitting the fabric

1   Dismantle the frame and lay the two webbing strips face down on two opposite sides of the fabric, making sure it lies on the straight grain.
2   Stitch through the fabric and webbing using backstitch and a strong thread.
3   Slot the rounded sides into place and roll until the fabric is tensioned, then tighten the wing nuts.
4   Lace the fabric to the flat sides with a strong thread to tension the fabric in both directions.

Stretchers

A simpler frame can be made by using artist's stretchers, which are available in many sizes. The sides are purchased in pairs of the desired length and, with tongue and groove ends, are just pushed together to make a frame.

Smaller stretchers, made especially for embroiderers, are also available, usually in an assorted pack. These are very useful for small projects. Alternatively, a home-made version can be made with 40 x 15mm (1⁹⁄₁₆ x ⅝in softwood batten, using angle brackets to hold the corners.

Fitting the fabric

1   Assemble the stretcher by pushing the corners together. Make sure the frame is square at the corners.
2   Using drawing pins or thumb tacks, pin the fabric along one of the longer sides, stretching the fabric slightly (*see* Fig 12.2).
3   Pin the opposite side, again stretching the fabric slightly and making sure that the grain of

165

Lay the fabric over the design and, with a fabric transfer pencil or soluble pen, trace the lines of the design onto the fabric.

Embroidery transfer pencils

The purpose of a transfer pencil is to create a transfer – to trace a design onto paper which can then be ironed off onto fabric. Transfer pencils can also be used directly onto fabric. The pencil line will wash out after use.

Always have a very sharp point as this gives a fine line which will be hidden by the stitching and may not need to be washed out when the stitching is finished.

Remember that if the iron-off method is used, the design will appear in reverse.

Soluble pens

Water-soluble and air-soluble pens are widely used by embroiderers. They are similar to a felt-tip pen, and usually give a pink or blue line.

Water-soluble ink can be removed with a damp cotton bud or by washing the complete item if required.

Air-soluble pens should only be used for pieces or sections of pieces that will not take long to work, as the ink disappears within a few hours.

Photocopies

A design can be photocopied and the resulting copy then ironed off onto fabric. This works best on fabrics of natural fibres such as cotton and silk. Some synthetics are resistant, but it is always worth trying.

Obviously, this method reverses the design, but it does have the advantage of being very quick and simple.

Colour photocopies

A colour photocopy can be made directly onto fabric or canvas. This is very helpful for producing 'tapestries' or wall hangings with intricate designs. Calico is a good base, though for designs that are to be embroidered on counted thread, an evenweave or canvas is required.

Designs can usually be enlarged or reduced on a photocopier, so it is possible to achieve the exact scale.

With the design photocopied onto the fabric, the embroidery can be worked as if on a printed canvas, in tent or cross stitch.

13 Bonding methods and colouring techniques

There are several safe methods of using adhesive bonding agents to facilitate the making of miniature items. These agents are available due to the development of modern plastic-based adhesives.

The adhesive webs on interlinings and Bond-a-web will not harm fabrics as they are stable and do not change over time. Most of the fabric glues available are PVA-based and, like the various craft and wood glues, will not harm fabric or change once dry. Avoid using latex-based glues as these *will* change with time, eventually staining the fabric.

Fabric glues remain flexible after use whereas craft and wood glues dry stiff.

Using fabric paints or dyes on basic linen or canvas can be an advantage when making very small miniature items: the use of colour removes the need to work the whole of the background, thus eliminating unnecessary bulk.

Fabric dyes and paints allow any colour to be achieved, which can be particularly important if you want an antique look as the rather brightly coloured evenweaves that are commercially available do not always enable this.

Adhesives and Interlinings

Adhesives

Only PVA-based glues are suitable for use with fabric. There are many different types available. White PVA glues range from children's glue, which is the most dilute version, to paper glue, wallpaper adhesive and extra strong wood glue. All can be diluted with water.

PVA wood glue, even when diluted, dries fairly stiff and can be used to stiffen fabric. PVA fabric glues, however, dry flexible and can be used to prevent fabric fraying. Avoid wallpaper adhesive as it usually contains a fungicide which can have an adverse effect on the fabric after a period of time. Also avoid using latex-based glues which, after some time, tend to yellow and return to being sticky.

Bond-a-web

This is the brand name for a web of adhesive which is supported by non-stick paper. It can be used to bond two fabrics or to bond fabric to paper or card.

Place the Bond-a-web on the reverse side of the fabric with the adhesive next to the fabric (i.e., paper side uppermost). Press with an iron set to the correct heat for the fabric being used, then remove the paper backing. The fabric can then be turned over and bonded in the same way to another surface.

It is a good idea to have one piece of non-stick baking paper on the ironing surface and another between the iron and the piece being bonded, to protect the work surface and the iron.

Bonding powder

This is a powdered form of the adhesive used in Bond-a-web. It is used by embroiderers when small or scattered areas are to be bonded for creative effects.

Sprinkle the powder over the fabric surface then add the desired small fragments of thread or fabric. Place a sheet of non-stick paper over the whole surface and press with an iron as above.

Bonded interlinings

There are several brands of bonded interlining available; some are woven and some, like vilene, are fused. The interlining has a web of adhesive on one side which can be used to stiffen fabric or bond two fabrics together.

Interlinings are available in various weights, from ultra-light to pelmet weight. They are used in the same way as Bond-a-web, by pressing with an iron set to the correct heat for the fabric being used.

Fabric Dyes and Paints

There are many different types of fabric paint and dye available. Some are for use on particular fabrics, including dyes for silk, dyes for natural fibres and dyes for synthetics. Such dyes are washable when used correctly on the fabric for which they are intended. However, if the item is never going to be washed, as is the case with most miniature pieces, any dyes or paints can be used on any fabric – even artists' watercolours.

When colouring a small area, the fabric dye or paint is best applied with a brush rather than by immersing the fabric. Place the fabric into a frame so that it is tight and smooth, and paint on the dye or paint with a small brush. Leave the fabric to dry in the frame, on a level surface, so that the dye dries evenly.

Some fabrics have a high level of natural oils or dressing, for example linen, and require more than one application of colour.

A completed piece of work can be 'antiqued' by painting on a solution of cold black tea. Always test this on a spare piece of fabric first, to make sure you are happy with the resultant colour.

Fabric transfer paints

There are several brands of transfer paints available, all with the word 'transfer' somewhere on the label. They are all made for use on synthetic fabrics, on which they give the brightest colours. When used on natural fibres, the colours are softer.

Transfer paints and dyes are first painted onto paper and then ironed off on to fabric. Remember that this reverses the design.

There is a considerable difference between the colours when they have been painted on paper and when they have been ironed off. For this reason, a sample strip should be made first to see how the colour will appear on the fabric before using it on the actual piece.

A photocopy of the design can be painted and ironed off or a tracing onto detail paper can be used. Actual tracing paper is not successful. Detail paper, sometimes sold in 'marker pads', is a white, opaque paper that can be seen through when placed over a design.

When ironing off the transfer, move the iron gently and smoothly so that the paper remains in the same place. It may take several minutes to transfer onto some fabrics.

14 Finishing methods

Counted thread embroidery on linen or canvas often distorts. The use of a frame will prevent this to a certain extent, but the completed embroidery often needs to be blocked back into shape. This must be done before the excess fabric or canvas is removed and before a hem is formed.

In miniature work especially, unnecessary thickness and bulk must be avoided and removing excess fabric to work a mitred corner is one way of achieving this.

Blocking embroidery

Before blocking, make sure all the threads used are colourfast, and test any painted backgrounds to make sure the dyes were fixed. Moisten a small area and blot with a tissue to see if any colour transfers.

Working method

1 Draw a rectangle on the paper using the waterproof pen. Make sure all the corners are true right angles. This rectangle should be larger than the piece of embroidery to be blocked. The pen lines will provide straight edges to follow.

2 Lay the paper on the pinboard and cover it with the sheet of plastic.

3 Trim the excess fabric, on the straight grain.

4 With a small damp cloth or sponge, dampen the embroidery and the surrounding canvas or linen.

5 Lay the embroidery within the paper rectangle and begin pinning the fabric to the board, from the middle of one side to the corner, stretching the fabric slightly as you work. Use the line on the paper as a guide.

6 Return to the middle of the side and work towards the other corner in the same way.

7 Repeat the process along the opposite side.

8 Repeat again with the two remaining sides.

9 Leave the piece to dry naturally, laying flat on a surface in an even temperature and covered lightly with tissue paper.

10 When completely dry, remove the pins. If the original piece was very badly distorted, a second blocking may be needed.

Blocking

Materials

Pinboard or similar, soft enough for
    drawing pins or thumb tacks
Paper
Transparent plastic sheeting
Drawing pins or thumb tacks
Waterproof pen

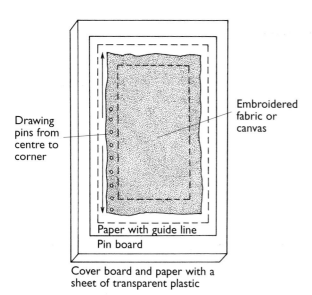

Fig 14.1 **Blocking a completed piece of canvaswork.**

Mitred corners

The method given below will give a neat finish and removes excess fabric.

Working method

1 Trim the seam allowance.

2 Cut a small amount from the corner of the fabric.

3 Fold the corner down diagonally.

4 Fold the adjacent sides once, and then again, and secure with tiny hemming stitches.

Fig 14.2 **Making a mitred corner.**

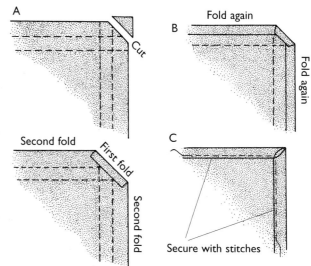

Fastening on

The old rule that 'thou shalt not start with a knot' derives from a time when most embroidered articles had to be laundered, and a knot would unravel in the washing process.

When making miniatures, which are unlikely to need repeated washing, it is sometimes an advantage to begin with a small knot. However, the best method, once some stitching has been worked, is to secure the beginning of the thread into the back of the existing stitching.

On an evenweave fabric or canvas use the following method.

Take the thread, knotted at the end, through from the front of the fabric, a little distance from the starting point and in advance of the immediate stitching area. As the stitching progresses towards the knot, the stitches will cover the thread that is lying on the back of the work. The knot on the front of the work can then be cut off as the existing stitching will hold the end on the reverse side.

Another method of fastening on is described under Darning on Net (*see* page 176).

Backstitch

Backstitch is used for working a line.

Bring the needle through from the back of the fabric and take it down again to give the length of stitch required. Bring the needle up through the fabric again, the length of a stitch away from the previous stitch (at A), then take the needle back through the fabric, next to the previous stitch (B).

When complete, fasten off into the back of the stitches.

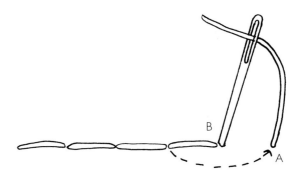

Blanket or buttonhole stitch

These stitches can be used to form an edging or a row of stitching, and can be radiated to form a flower effect.

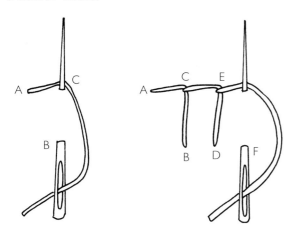

For blanket stitch, bring the needle through from the back of the fabric at A, and take it down at B, a little to one side of A, to give the desired length and direction of stitch. Bring the needle back through at C, in line with B, making sure the thread is behind the needle. Continue in this way, taking the needle down at D, to the right or left of C, and up at E, in line with D, keeping the thread behind the needle.

When complete, fasten off into the back of the stitches.

Buttonhole stitch is worked in the same way, but with the stitches very close together.

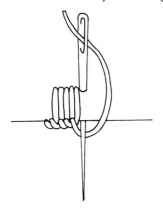

Couching

In couching, a thread is laid on the surface of the fabric and stitched down with a second, finer thread.

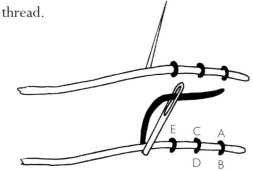

Bring the thread to be laid through from the back of the fabric. Threaded in a second needle, bring the sewing thread through from the back, immediately beside the first thread (A), and take a stitch over the first thread and down close to the other side (B). Continue to secure the first thread in this manner, at the same time moving the first thread, if necessary, to form the shape or line required.

Fasten the sewing thread off behind the stitching, then take the first thread through to the back and fasten it off.

Cross stitch

The diagram shows the method for working a row of cross stitch by making the first half of each stitch all the way along the row and then

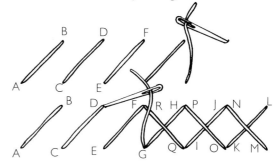

working the second half on the way back along the row.

For the first row, bring the needle up at A, down at B, up at C, down at D and so on until the row is as long as you require. Then, work back along the row crossing over these first stitches, by bringing the needle up at M, down at N, up at O, down at P and so on, until all the stitches have been crossed.

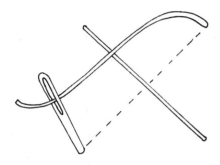

A second method is to work each cross stitch in full as you go. For one stitch, following the diagram, bring the needle up at K, down at L, up at M and down at N.

It depends on the design or pattern as to which method is chosen.

Fasten off in the back of the stitching.

Darning

For this stitch a tapestry needle must be used. In this book darning is used only on evenweave fabrics or canvas to facilitate counting. It produces a regular pattern.

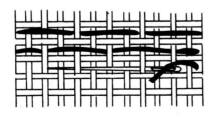

Bring the needle through from the back of the fabric and take it down again, having passed over the required number of threads. Pass under the required number of threads before bringing the needle up again, and continue in this way to the end of the row. In the diagram, the thread is passed over three and under one.

Usually, rows of stitches are worked in every row of holes in the fabric/canvas, though empty rows can be left in between.

Fasten off into the back of the stitching.

Darning on net

Darning stitch on net is worked by weaving the thread through the holes in the net fabric to form the required pattern.

Photocopy, trace or draw the design on paper, and tack the piece of net into position over the design.

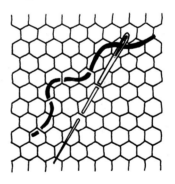

Begin by taking the needle through the holes of the net, leaving an end of about 25mm (1in). Proceed to darn in and out of the holes, following the design. For miniature work, always darn in and out of adjacent holes.

When an area is complete, simply cut the thread off close to the net and leave, trimming the starting end in the same way. When   the whole design is complete, remove the netting from the paper pattern and cut the item to shape.

Detached chain stitch

This stitch is useful for working flowers and leaves. Working a short stitch produces a rounded shape while a longer stitch produces a narrower oval shape.

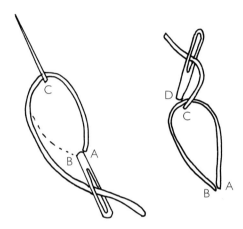

Bring the needle through from the back of the fabric (A), then take it down as close as possible to the same point (B). Bring the needle up again at C, making a stitch of the length required, and looping the thread under the needle. Pull the thread through and take a small stitch over the loop to secure it (D).

When complete, fasten off in the back of the stitching.

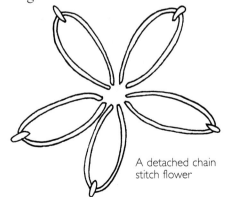

A detached chain stitch flower

Feather stitch

Feather stitching can be used to give a decorative outline or edging.

Bring the needle through from the back of the fabric to come up at A, and take it down at B. Before pulling the thread through, bring the needle up again at C and loop the thread under the needle. Draw the thread through. Take the needle down at D and up at E in the same way, again looping the thread under the needle. Continue in this way until the required number of stitches have been worked.

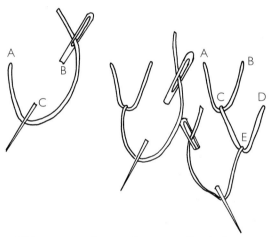

When complete, take a small stitch over the last loop to secure.

French knot

This stitch can be used alone or in clusters. They add texture to a piece.

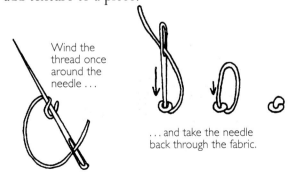

Wind the thread once around the needle . . .

. . . and take the needle back through the fabric.

Bring the needle through from the back of the fabric and wind the thread once around the needle. Take the point of the needle back through the fabric, very close to where the thread was brought through to the front. Draw the thread through to form a neat, compact knot.

Hemming

Hemming stitch is used to secure hems.

Turn the edge of the fabric over as desired. Pick up a little of the fabric and the turned hem with the needle and draw the thread through, repeating until all of the hem has been secured. Only a tiny stitch should show on the right side, so it is an advantage to use a very fine needle.

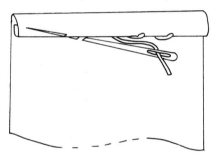

Herringbone stitch

Herringbone stitch is generally used to give a decorative border, but can also be used as a filling stitch.

Bring the needle through from the back of the fabric to come up at A, then take it down at

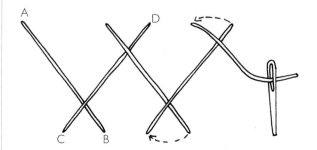

B to form a diagonal stitch. Bring the needle back up at C, to one side of B, then make another diagonal stitch to cross over the first. Continue in this way until the desired number of stitches have been worked.

Fasten off into the back of the stitching.

Running stitch

This is basically the same as darning, but is worked on plain fabric rather than a counted fabric, and the spaces and stitches are of equal length. It is used for outlining and in quilting.

Length of space is equivalent to length of stitch

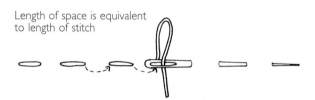

Take the needle in and out of the fabric to form stitches and spaces, all of a uniform length, in the line or shape required.

Satin stitch

This stitch is used as a filling for small areas.

Bring the needle through from the back of the fabric, at a point on the outline at one end of the shape to be filled. Take the needle back through the fabric on the opposite side of the shape, and then up again very close to the first stitch. Continue to place stitches next to one

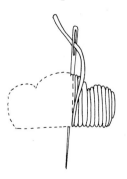

another in this manner until the shape is filled.

Fasten off into the back of the stitching.

Seeding stitches

Seeding is an effect created by short, straight stitches scattered at various angles. Traditionally, two stitches are used side by side, but for miniature work a single stitch is sufficient.

Simply work short stitches of equal length at angles to each other, clustered together.

Straight stitch

Straight stitch is the most basic and versatile embroidery stitch. It can be used for outlining and filling in and for tiny leaves or flowers. It is simply a single stitch which can be of any length, and used side by side or angled to radiate.

Bring the needle through from the back of the fabric and take it down again to make a stitch of the length required. Continue laying stitches in this way to form the outline or shape that you require.

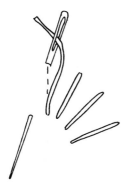

Tent stitch

By using tent stitch rather than half cross stitch, the stitches can be worked in any direction and look exactly the same on the front. Tent stitch also prevents the thread from slipping behind the weave of the fabric and disappearing as it tends to with half cross stitch.

The diagram shows the sequence of stitches for working in different directions. Bring the needle through from the back of the fabric at the odd numbers and take it down through the even numbers. The top diagram shows the placing of the needle.

When working rows next to one another, use the same holes as the previous row – do not leave a thread of canvas empty in between.

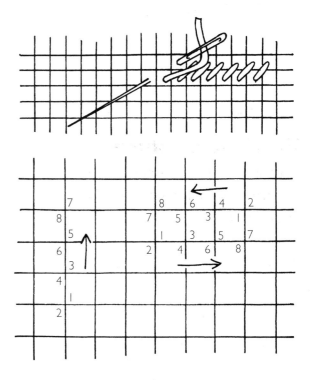

Sources of Information

Museums

Most large towns and cities have a museum with a display of decorative arts that includes embroidered items. Many museums cover social history, showing the way people lived and the artifacts they used in their everyday lives. Some even have authentic room settings with furnishings of a particular period. Such things provide valuable general information.

If you want specific information, it is best to write to the curator in advance, stating exactly what you wish to know. A short list of clear questions will almost always bring a prompt response, but a general 'Tell me all you know about beds/chairs/Victorian houses/etc' rarely gets a reply.

In most countries, a list of museums and historical houses is published, usually updated every couple of years or so. Libraries have copies of these or lists of their own, and sometimes a section devoted to local history.

The brief list which follows is a starting point, indicating museums which have collections of Victorian historical embroidery and, in some cases, furnishings.

United Kingdom and Ireland

Geffrye Museum
Kingsland Road
London E2 8EA
0171 739 8368/9893

Room settings.

The Embroiderers' Guild
Apartment 41
Hampton Court Palace
East Molesey
Surrey KT8 9AU
0181 943 1229

Historical embroidery.
(By appointment only.)
The Guild have branches throughout the UK and Ireland, the USA, Canada and Australia.

Victoria and Albert Museum
Cromwell Road
London SW7
0171 938 8500

Embroidery, costume and furniture.

William Morris Gallery
The Water House
Lloyd Park
Forest Road
Walthamstow
London E17
0181 527 3782

Arts and Crafts textiles and furnishings.

Bowes Museum
Barnard Castle
Co. Durham DL12 8NP
01833 690606

Embroidery, costume and furnishings.

The American Museum
Claverton Manor
Bath
Avon BA2 7BD
01225 460503

Room settings.

Fitzwilliam Museum
Trumpington Street
Cambridge
Cambridgeshire CB2 1RB
01223 332900

Embroidery, mostly samplers.

Guildford Museum
Castle Arch
Guildford
Surrey GU1 3SX
01483 444750

Embroidery.

Maidstone Museum and Art Gallery
St Faith's Street
Maidstone
Kent ME14 1LH
01622 754497

Embroidery and furnishings.

Whitworth Art Gallery
University of Manchester
Oxford Road
Manchester
Greater Manchester M15 6ER
0161 275 7450

Fabrics and furnishings.

Costume Museum
51 Castlegate
Nottingham
Nottinghamshire NG1 6AF
0115 915 3500/5555

Costume, embroidery and lace.

York Castle Museum
The Eye of York
York
Yorkshire YO1 9RY
01904 653611

Room settings.

Royal Museum
Chambers Street
Edinburgh EH1 1JF
Scotland
0131 225 7534

Embroidery and furnishings.

The Burrell Collection
Pollok Country Park
2060 Pollokshaws Road
Glasgow G43 1AT
Scotland
0141 649 7151

Embroideries and tapestries.

Cardiff Castle
Castle Street
Cardiff CF1 2RB
South Glamorgan
01222 878 100

Arts and Crafts movement furniture and artifacts.

Ulster Folk and Transport Museum
153 Bangor Road
Cultra
Holywood
Co. Down BT18 0EU
Northern Ireland
01232 428428

Textiles and crafts.

Ulster Museum
Botanic Gardens
Stranmillis Road
Belfast BT9 5AB
Northern Ireland
01232 383000

Costume and lace.

Art Nouveau room setting.

National Museum of Ireland
Kildare Street and
7–9 Merrion Row
 and Merrion Street
Dublin 2
Republic of Ireland
003531 6777 444

Decorative arts and lace.

United States of America and Canada

The Baltimore Museum of Art
Art Museum Drive
Baltimore
Maryland 21218
410 396 6300

Quilts and household items.

Museum of Fine Arts
465 Huntington Avenue
Boston
Massachusetts 02115
617 267 9300

Large collection of textiles.

The Art Institute of Chicago
Michigan Avenue
 at Adams Street
Chicago
Illinois 60603
312 443 3600

Large collection of textiles.

The Farmers' Museum and Fenimore House
PO Box 800
Cooperstown
New York 13326
607 547 1450

Bedcovers and carpets.

Historic Deerfield Inc.
PO Box 321
Deerfield
Massachusetts 01342
413 774 5581

Household items.

Indianapolis Museum of Art
1200 West 38th Street
Indianapolis
Indiana 46208
317 923 1331

Eighteenth and nineteenth century embroidery.

The Brooklyn Museum
200 Eastern Parkway
Brooklyn
New York City
New York 11238
718 638 5000

Costume, bedhangings and window hangings.

The Metropolitan Museum of Art
1000 Fifth Avenue
5th Avenue at 82nd Street
New York City
New York 10028
212 879 5500

Costume and embroidery.

Philadelphia Museum of Art
Box 7646
Philadelphia
Pennsylvania 19101
215 763 8100

American and English embroideries.

National Museum of History and Technology
Smithsonian Institution
14th Street and Constitution Avenue
Washington DC 20560
202 357 2700

Coverlets and embroideries.

Royal Ontario Museum
100 Queens Park
Toronto
Ontario M5S 2C6
416 586 5549

Large collection of embroidery and lace.

Note: Many Canadian museums specialize in folk textiles, but may have small collections of Victorian embroidery.

Historic Houses

These houses, which are well documented in books, magazines and libraries, are a good source of reference. Some are dedicated and restored to one particular era, but many have been added to over the centuries. Textiles, furnishings and sometimes embroideries are shown in context within room settings.

In most countries there are heritage organizations to care for these estates and houses, such as the National Trust and English Heritage in the United Kingdom. Please consult telephone directories and Tourist Information Offices for information on local organizations and houses.

Booklets or postcards from these organizations are usually available.

Books

Information and illustrations on embroidery, interior decoration, restoring period houses, furniture and decorative art styles can be found in books. There are also many specialist periodicals available which cover these areas. Your local reference library, or a browse in a large book shop, are good starting points.

The brief list which follows includes some books which may be out of print, but can be seen at libraries or purchased from secondhand book dealers.

Parry, Linda, *William Morris Textiles*, Weidenfeld and Nicolson Ltd, London, UK, 1983
ISBN 0297 78196 0

Johnson, Pauline, *Three Hundred Years of Embroidery, 1600–1900*, Wakefield Press in association with the Embroiderers' Guild of South Australia and The Embroiderers' Guild, Hampton Court Palace, Surrey, 1987
ISBN 0949268 81X

Benn, Elizabeth (Editor), *Treasures from the Embroiderers' Guild Collection*, David & Charles, Devon, UK, 1991
ISBN 07153 9829 6

Miller, Judith and Martin, *Period Details*, Mitchell Beazley, London, UK, 1988
ISBN 085533 6501

Miller, Judith and Martin, *Victorian Style*, Mitchell Beazley, London, UK, 1994
ISBN 185732 0980

Swain, Margaret, *Scottish Embroidery, Medieval to Modern*, B.T. Batsford Ltd, London, UK, 1986
ISBN 07134 4638 2

Warner, Pamela, *Embroidery: A History*, B.T. Batsford Ltd, London, UK, 1991
ISBN 07134 61063

About the author

Pamela Warner's interest in embroidery began in the mid-1950s with her studies for a National Design Diploma (NDD) in fashion – which included embroidery – at Bromley College of Art.

After a career in banking and computing, followed by marriage and a family, Pamela rediscovered creative embroidery at an evening class. She went on to qualify and by 1979 was teaching embroidery for Bromley Adult Education and the Inner London Education Authority (ILEA). During the early 1980s she became involved as a tutor for City and Guilds embroidery classes at Bromley, and eventually took on full responsibility for the course. This continues to be her main occupation, along with working as an external verifier for the City and Guilds examination board.

Pamela discovered dolls' houses in 1989. She began with a ready-made house and a kit, but was soon frustrated with the small rooms. In order to learn the craft herself, she went on a Dolls' House Holiday, with Peter Alden, and was so impressed with the results that she keeps returning (seven holidays by 1997).

Pamela's work as a professional embroiderer has been exhibited widely, and she has undertaken many commissions for ecclesiastic and secular pieces. She has also spent 15 years restoring and conserving embroideries for Westminster Abbey and various other churches.

This is Pamela's second book, following *Embroidery: A History* and a series of booklets on the history of embroidery.

Index

'Abide with me' samplers
118–19,120
adhesives 169, 170
Aesthetic movement 6
air-soluble pens 168
Alphabet sampler 118, 120
appliqué, mock 77–8, 136–7
Art Needlework 4, 113
Art Nouveau style 5
    cushion 64–5
    footstool 90–2
    screen 104–5
Arts and Crafts Movement 3,5, 37
    carpet 16–18
    curtains 47–50

backstitch 174
beaded curtains 54–6
beads (for filling cushions) 80
bedcovers 122–44
    determining size 123
bell pulls 148–50
Berlin Wool Work 3, 4, 113
Bird on a Branch picture 114–15
blanket stitch 175
block patchwork 70–5, 127–31
blocking embroidery 10, 172–3
Bond-a-web 170
bonded interlinings 170
bonding powder 170
books 183
buttonhole stitch 175

canvas: preparation 12
canvaswork
    chair seats 84–6
    cushions 58–62
    pictures 114–16
    rugs 32–5
carbon, dressmakers' 167
card mounts 166
carpets 10–24
Cat cushion 58–60
chair seats 81–6
Clanfield cushion 63–4
cold-water soluble fabric 54
colour photocopies 168
commercial pleater 38, 40
corners, mitred 173
couched rugs 26–7
couching 175
    cushion edges 80, 81
counted thread work 161
crazy patchwork 67, 68, 123–4
cross stitch 175–6
curtains 36–56
    pleating 38–40
    positioning and sizing 37–8
cushions 57–81
    alternative edgings 80, 81
    filling 80
    making up 79–80

darned rugs 29–31
darning 176
    on net 51–2, 176–7
designs, transferring 167–8
detached chain stitch 177
detail paper 171
draped pelmets 42–4
dressmakers' carbon 167
dyes, fabric 169, 171

early Victorian style 3, 36
    carpet 11–13
edgings for cushions 80, 81
Edwardian style 5–6
    cushion 66–7
    screen 104–5
embroidered bedspread 141–4
embroidered curtains 47–50
embroidered screens 101–5
embroidery frames 164–7
embroidery transfer pencils 168

fabric fringes 19
fabric paints/dyes 169, 171
    transfer paints 77, 134–5, 171
fastening on 174
feather stitch 177
filling cushions 80
finishing methods 172–3
fire screens 94, 100
Florentine chair seats 82–3
Flower Pot cushion 63–4
Foam-Cor 39
folding screens 94, 100, 106–7
footstools 86–93
    making up 92–3
frames, embroidery 164–7
framing pictures/samplers 120–1
French knot 177–8
fringes 19–20, 31

Garland designs 61–2, 86–90
gathering by hand 38–9
geometric patterns, printed 77
Geometric screen 98, 99
Gothic Revival 3, 5, 122
Grisaille design 61–2, 88–9

hanging letter cases 158–9
hemming stitch 178
hems
    carpets 18
    table covers 110–11
herringbone stitch 178
hexagon patchwork 68–9,125–6
historic houses 183
home-made pleater 38, 39
'Home Sweet Home' samplers 118,
    119, 120
hot-water soluble fabric 54

influences on design/style 2–7
interlinings, bonded 170

kapok 80
knotted fringes 19–20

lace curtains 50–4
lace table mats/runners 111–12
lace-trimmed hem 110
late Victorian style 4
    carpet 14–15
letter cases 158–9
linen table cloth 109
Little House on the Prairie
    patchwork
    72–3, 129–30
Log Cabin patchwork 74–5, 130–1

machine embroidering 52–4
Mackintosh, Charles Rennie 5, 7
mantel valances 146–8
mats, table 111–12
mitred corners 173
mock appliqué 77–8, 136–7
Morris, William 3, 5, 7, 16,
    32–3,113
    embroidered bedspread 141–4
    embroidered cushions 63–4
    footstool 90–2
    Morris-style screen 101–3
Multicoloured House/Motif
    sampler
    118, 119–20
museums 180–2

needlework boxes 150–4
net: darning on 51–2, 176–7
nightdress cases 159–60
Nine-Patch design 70–1, 127–8

Oval Posy design 86–7, 95–6
oversewn edge 80, 81

paints, fabric 169, 171
    transfer paints 77, 134–5, 171
patchwork
    bedcovers 123–6
    block 70–5, 127–31
    cushions 67–9
    simulated 76–7, 132–5
Peacock screen 96–7
pelmets 40–4
photocopies 168
pictures 113–16, 120–1
plaited rugs 26, 27, 28–9
pleating curtains 38–40
plush stitch 4
pole screens 94, 98–100
Posy design 61–2, 86–7
pot stands 157
printed fabrics 77, 132–3
PVA-based glues 170

quilting
    bedcovers 122, 123, 137–40
    cushions 78–9

rag rugs 31–2
Rose Spray cushion 58–60
rugs 25–35
Ruin and Waterfall picture 114–16
runners, table 111–12
running stitch 178

samplers 113, 117–21
satin stitch 178–9
scale 9
    working to 1/24 scale 161–3
screens 94–107
    making up 98–100, 106–7
seeding stitches 179
simulated patchwork 76–7, 132–5
slate frames 165
small decorative items 145–60
small 'lace' items 111–12
soluble fabric 52
    dissolving 54
soluble pens 168
spring frames 167
stair carpets 20–4
stitches 174–9
straight stitch 179
stretchers 165–6
striped fabrics 76–7, 133

table covers/linen 108–12
    adjusting pattern size 109
    draping cloths 111
tails 44, 45
tambours 166–7
tassels 46
    'mock' for cushions 80, 81
tent stitch 179
tie-backs 44–6
trace and tack 167
tracing through fabric 167–8
transfer paints 77, 134–5, 171
transfer pencils 168
transferring designs 167–8

valances, mantel 146–8
Vase cushion 58–9
'Verse' sampler 118–19

wadding 80
watch pockets 154–6
water-soluble pens 168

Titles available from
GMC PUBLICATIONS

BOOKS

Woodworking

40 More Woodworking Plans & Projects	*GMC Publications*	Making Little Boxes from Wood	*John Bennett*
Bird Boxes and Feeders for the Garden	*Dave Mackenzie*	Making Shaker Furniture	*Barry Jackson*
Complete Woodfinishing	*Ian Hosker*	Pine Furniture Projects for the Home	*Dave Mackenzie*
Electric Woodwork	*Jeremy Broun*	The Router and Furniture & Cabinetmaking	
Furniture & Cabinetmaking Projects	*GMC Publications*	Test Reports	*GMC Publications*
Furniture Projects	*Rod Wales*	Sharpening Pocket Reference Book	*Jim Kingshott*
Furniture Restoration (Practical Crafts)	*Kevin Jan Bonner*	Sharpening: The Complete Guide	*Jim Kingshott*
Furniture Restoration and Repair for Beginners	*Kevin Jan Bonner*	Space-Saving Furniture Projects	*Dave Mackenzie*
Green Woodwork	*Mike Abbott*	Stickmaking: A Complete Course	*Andrew Jones & Clive George*
The Incredible Router	*Jeremy Broun*	Veneering: A Complete Course	*Ian Hosker*
Making & Modifying Woodworking Tools	*Jim Kingshott*	Woodfinishing Handbook (Practical Crafts)	*Ian Hosker*
Making Chairs and Tables	*GMC Publications*	Woodworking Plans and Projects	*GMC Publications*
Making Fine Furniture	*Tom Darby*	The Workshop	*Jim Kingshott*

Woodturning

Adventures in Woodturning	*David Springett*	Practical Tips for Turners & Carvers	*GMC Publications*
Bert Marsh: Woodturner	*Bert Marsh*	Practical Tips for Woodturners	*GMC Publications*
Bill Jones' Notes from the Turning Shop	*Bill Jones*	Spindle Turning	*GMC Publications*
Bill Jones' Further Notes from the Turning Shop	*Bill Jones*	Turning Miniatures in Wood	*John Sainsbury*
Colouring Techniques for Woodturners	*Jan Sanders*	Turning Wooden Toys	*Terry Lawrence*
The Craftsman Woodturner	*Peter Child*	Understanding Woodturning	*Ann & Bob Phillips*
Decorative Techniques for Woodturners	*Hilary Bowen*	Useful Techniques for Woodturners	*GMC Publications*
Essential Tips for Woodturners	*GMC Publications*	Useful Woodturning Projects	*GMC Publications*
Faceplate Turning	*GMC Publications*	Woodturning: A Foundation Course	*Keith Rowley*
Fun at the Lathe	*R.C. Bell*	Woodturning: A Source Book of Shapes	*John Hunnex*
Illustrated Woodturning Techniques	*John Hunnex*	Woodturning Jewellery	*Hilary Bowen*
Intermediate Woodturning Projects	*GMC Publications*	Woodturning Masterclass	*Tony Boase*
Keith Rowley's Woodturning Projects	*Keith Rowley*	Woodturning Techniques	*GMC Publications*
Make Money from Woodturning	*Ann & Bob Phillips*	Woodturning Tools & Equipment Test Reports	*GMC Publications*
Multi-Centre Woodturning	*Ray Hopper*	Woodturning Wizardry	*David Springett*
Pleasure and Profit from Woodturning	*Reg Sherwin*		

Woodcarving

The Art of the Woodcarver	*GMC Publications*	Understanding Woodcarving in the Round	*GMC Publications*
Carving Birds & Beasts	*GMC Publications*	Useful Techniques for Woodcarvers	*GMC Publications*
Carving on Turning	*Chris Pye*	Wildfowl Carving - Volume 1	*Jim Pearce*
Carving Realistic Birds	*David Tippey*	Wildfowl Carving - Volume 2	*Jim Pearce*
Decorative Woodcarving	*Jeremy Williams*	The Woodcarvers	*GMC Publications*
Essential Tips for Woodcarvers	*GMC Publications*	Woodcarving: A Complete Course	*Ron Butterfield*
Essential Woodcarving Techniques	*Dick Onians*	Woodcarving: A Foundation Course	*Zoë Gertner*
Lettercarving in Wood: A Practical Course	*Chris Pye*	Woodcarving for Beginners	*GMC Publications*
Practical Tips for Turners & Carvers	*GMC Publications*	Woodcarving Tools & Equipment Test Reports	*GMC Publications*
Relief Carving in Wood: A Practical Introduction	*Chris Pye*	Woodcarving Tools, Materials & Equipment	*Chris Pye*
Understanding Woodcarving	*GMC Publications*		

Upholstery

Seat Weaving (Practical Crafts)	*Ricky Holdstock*	Upholstery Restoration	*David James*
Upholsterer's Pocket Reference Book	*David James*	Upholstery Techniques & Projects	*David James*
Upholstery: A Complete Course	*David James*		

Toymaking

Designing & Making Wooden Toys	*Terry Kelly*	Restoring Rocking Horses	*Clive Green & Anthony Dew*
Fun to Make Wooden Toys & Games	*Jeff & Jennie Loader*	Scrollsaw Toy Projects	*Ivor Carlyle*
Making Board, Peg & Dice Games	*Jeff & Jennie Loader*	Wooden Toy Projects	*GMC Publications*
Making Wooden Toys & Games	*Jeff & Jennie Loader*		

Dolls' Houses and Miniatures

Architecture for Dolls' Houses	*Joyce Percival*	Making Period Dolls' House Accessories	*Andrea Barham*
Beginners' Guide to the Dolls' House Hobby	*Jean Nisbett*	Making Period Dolls' House Furniture	*Derek & Sheila Rowbottom*
The Complete Dolls' House Book	*Jean Nisbett*	Making Tudor Dolls' Houses	*Derek Rowbottom*
Dolls' House Accessories, Fixtures and Fittings	*Andrea Barham*	Making Unusual Miniatures	*Graham Spalding*
Dolls' House Bathrooms: Lots of Little Loos	*Patricia King*	Making Victorian Dolls' House Furniture	*Patricia King*
Easy to Make Dolls' House Accessories	*Andrea Barham*	Miniature Bobbin Lace	*Roz Snowden*
Make Your Own Dolls' House Furniture	*Maurice Harper*	Miniature Embroidery for the Victorian Dolls' House	*Pamela Warner*
Making Dolls' House Furniture	*Patricia King*	Miniature Needlepoint Carpets	*Janet Granger*
Making Georgian Dolls' Houses	*Derek Rowbottom*	The Secrets of the Dolls' House Makers	*Jean Nisbett*
Making Miniature Oriental Rugs & Carpets	*Meik & Ian McNaughton*		

Crafts

American Patchwork Designs in Needlepoint	*Melanie Tacon*	Embroidery Tips & Hints	*Harold Hayes*
A Beginners' Guide to Rubber Stamping	*Brenda Hunt*	An Introduction to Crewel Embroidery	*Mave Glenny*
Celtic Knotwork Designs	*Sheila Sturrock*	Making Character Bears	*Valerie Tyler*
Collage from Seeds, Leaves and Flowers	*Joan Carver*	Making Greetings Cards for Beginners	*Pat Sutherland*
Complete Pyrography	*Stephen Poole*	Making Knitwear Fit	*Pat Ashforth & Steve Plummer*
Creating Knitwear Designs	*Pat Ashforth & Steve Plummer*	Needlepoint: A Foundation Course	*Sandra Hardy*
Creative Embroidery Techniques Using		Pyrography Handbook (Practical Crafts)	*Stephen Poole*
Colour Through Gold	*Daphne J. Ashby & Jackie Woolsey*	Tassel Making for Beginners	*Enid Taylor*
Cross Stitch Kitchen Projects	*Janet Granger*	Tatting Collage	*Lindsay Rogers*
Cross Stitch on Colour	*Sheena Rogers*	Temari: A Traditional Japanese Embroidery Technique	*Margaret Ludlow*

The Home

Home Ownership: Buying and Maintaining	*Nicholas Snelling*	Security for the Householder: Fitting Locks and Other Devices	*E. Phillips*

VIDEOS

Drop-in and Pinstuffed Seats	*David James*	Twists and Advanced Turning	*Dennis White*
Stuffover Upholstery	*David James*	Sharpening the Professional Way	*Jim Kingshott*
Elliptical Turning	*David Springett*	Sharpening Turning & Carving Tools	*Jim Kingshott*
Woodturning Wizardry	*David Springett*	Bowl Turning	*John Jordan*
Turning Between Centres: The Basics	*Dennis White*	Hollow Turning	*John Jordan*
Turning Bowls	*Dennis White*	Woodturning: A Foundation Course	*Keith Rowley*
Boxes, Goblets and Screw Threads	*Dennis White*	Carving a Figure: The Female Form	*Ray Gonzalez*
Novelties and Projects	*Dennis White*	The Router: A Beginner's Guide	*Alan Goodsell*
Classic Profiles	*Dennis White*	The Scroll Saw: A Beginner's Guide	*John Burke*

MAGAZINES

WOODTURNING • WOODCARVING • FURNITURE & CABINETMAKING • THE ROUTER
THE DOLLS' HOUSE MAGAZINE • CREATIVE CRAFTS FOR THE HOME • BUSINESSMATTERS

The above represents a full list of all titles currently published or scheduled to be published.
All are available direct from the Publishers or through bookshops, newsagents and specialist retailers.
To place an order, or to obtain a complete catalogue, contact:

GMC Publications,
166 High Street, Lewes, East Sussex BN7 1XU, United Kingdom Tel: 01273 488005 Fax: 01273 478606

Orders by credit card are accepted